we can cook

D1529968

First edition for the United States, its territories and dependencies, and Canada published in 2011 by Barron's Educational Series, Inc.

Copyright © 2011 Elwin Street Productions
Conceived and produced by Elwin Street Productions
144 Liverpool Road
London N1 1 LA
United Kingdom
www.elwinstreet.com

All inquiries should be addressed to:
Barron's Educational Series, Inc.
250 Wireless Blvd.
Hauppauge, NY 11788
www.barronseduc.com

ISBN: 978-0-7641-6434-7
Library of Congress Control Number: 2011925526

The activities described in this book are to be carried out with parental supervision at all times. Every effort has been made to ensure the safety of the activities detailed. Neither the author nor the publishers shall be liable or responsible for any harm or damage done allegedly arising from any information or suggestion in this book.

Picture credits: Alamy: p. 101; Dreamstime: pp. 15, 59; Getty: Front cover, pp.13, 33, 66, 71, 86, 107, 119; iStock photos: back cover images, pp.8, 26, 79, 97, 108; Photolibrary: p. 63; Photos to go: p. 43

Illustrations: Isabel Alberdi
Recipe tester: Jo Bartell

Additional recipes supplied by: p. 54 Egg in a hole, Pediatric Nutrition Specialist Jill Castle, MS, RD, LDN; p. 114 Maco lassi ice pops, Tram Le, MS, RD, LD of Nutrition to Kitchen; p. 28 Sweet potato fries and p. 100 Fish sticks, Aviva Goldfarb, author and founder of The Six O'Clock Scramble® (www.thescramble.com)

Printed in China
9 8 7 6 5 4 3 2 1

we can cook

Introduce your child to the joy of cooking
with 75 simple recipes and activities

Jessica Fishman Levinson and Maja Pitamic

BARRON'S

Contents

Bread, pasta, and grains

Meat, chicken, fish, and tofu

Healthy treats

Introduction

As parents, we need to spend quality one-to-one time with our children and cooking presents a perfect opportunity, as it involves them in an everyday activity. Cooking with your child takes a little longer, and will probably be considerably messier, but it's a great bonding exercise.

From an early age children tend to have strong opinions, likes, and dislikes about food. I can well remember my niece as a baby being fed puréed spinach and the look of disgust on her face. It's not always easy to convince children to try new foods, or to choose the healthy option. Often, just involving them in the fun of cooking and creating their own meals, can encourage them to try new things. And possibly the thing that appeals the most to children about cooking is the creative aspect, when raw ingredients magically transform into a wonderful dish: Add a couple of ingredients to flour, and it can turn into so many different things!

Cooking also introduces children to a range of important skills, such as weighing, measuring, and pouring. You will also find in these pages a selection of food-related activities, including what foods are good for us, different tastes and textures, which cooking utensils to use,

and plenty more, so your children can have fun while they learn.

The recipes and activities here are designed for children and parents to do together, to help your children gain a positive understanding of food and cooking and while taking their first tentative steps in the kitchen. The recipes are intended to be healthy and nutritional (with an occasional sweet treat) but still appealing for young children. If your child has any food allergies, check the ingredients list carefully to see if any ingredients need to be substituted. For example, if your child is allergic to peanuts, you can use almond butter or soy nut butter in place. If your child has a milk allergy or is lactose intolerant, you can substitute soy-based or dairy-free products for milk and yogurt.

So let's help our children enjoy the simple fun of combining ingredients to create a healthy and delicious meal.

Safety and measurements

When cooking with children there are some steps you will have to do yourself for safety reasons and always bear in mind the following:

- ! Keep children away from open ovens, broiler pans and keep hot pans out of their reach. Remember that pans stay hot for a while after they have been removed from the stove.
- ! If your child is helping to stir something on the burner, be sure to supervise them at all times, and make sure they wear oven mitts.
- ! Be careful when sautéeing ingredients in oil, particularly when you are adding food to hot oil, as it can splatter and burn easily.
- ! Make sure you and your children wash hands with warm, soapy water both before and after touching raw chicken or eggs. Be careful that children don't stick their fingers in their mouths while working with raw chicken or eggs.
- ! Beware of sharp objects—supervise children when using knives or scissors. Let your children use a blunt or plastic knife to cut up softer items, but never a sharp knife.
- ! Make sure the blender or food processor is unplugged when adding the ingredients.
- ! Be careful of the pointy tip of skewers—break off the tip before serving to children.

Below are some common imperial to metric measurement conversions that are used in this book.

Weight

1 oz	25 g	11 oz	315 g
2 oz	60 g	12 oz	350 g
3 oz	85 g	13 oz	375 g
4 oz	115 g	14 oz	400 g
5 oz	150 g	15 oz	425 g
6 oz	175 g	16 oz (1 lb)	450 g
7 oz	200 g		
8 oz	225 g		
9 oz	255 g		
10 oz	280 g		

Volume

1 tsp	5 ml
1 tbsp	15 ml
1/4 cup	60 ml
1/3 cup	80 ml
1/2 cup	125 ml
2/3 cup	170 ml
3/4 cup	180 ml
1 cup	250 ml

Temperature

350°F	180°C
375°F	190°C
400°F	200°C
425°F	220°C

Length

1/2 inch	1.25 cm
1 inch	2.5 cm
2 inches	5.0 cm
3 inches	7.5 cm

1 Fruit

With all the many sweet and sugary treats available, the natural sweetness of many fruits doesn't have as strong an appeal for children's young tastebuds. These recipes are designed to present children with fruits in a fun way as well as introduce them to a range of new ones they may not have encountered before, so they will soon be happily consuming their fruit portions without fuss.

Baked bananas

1
serving

This easy, delicious baked banana recipe takes only a few minutes to prepare. Since bananas are naturally sweet, you don't need added sugar for this recipe to taste delicious. Bananas are chock-full of nutrients that are good for children—they contain fiber, vitamin C, which helps bruises heal faster, and are one of the best sources of potassium, which can protect the heart and decrease the risk of high blood pressure.

Ingredients

1 medium banana

2 tsp lemon juice

Cinnamon to taste

Equipment

A plastic knife

An oven-safe dish

1. Preheat the oven to 400°F. Have your child peel the banana and then cut it in half lengthwise, using a plastic knife.

2. Then, let her place the banana (cut side up) in an oven-safe dish, pour 1 teaspoon of lemon juice on each half and sprinkle with cinnamon.

3. Place the dish in the oven and bake for 10–15 minutes, depending on the texture you both prefer (the longer the banana bakes, the softer it gets).

4. Remove from the oven and serve.

Fruit picking

Picking fruit is a wonderful way to spend time outdoors with your child and the perfect opportunity to teach him about food that is good for him, and even the fussiest eaters seem perfectly happy to eat fruit that they've helped to pick themselves.

You will need

A nearby Pick Your Own farm, or similar

Containers for the fruit

Before you go, check which fruits are in season. Explain to your child that the availability of a particular fruit changes according to the season. The summer months are the best time to go— you'll find fruit such as strawberries, raspberries, blueberries, cherries, pears, and plums.

   When picking the fruit, ask him to look at all the differences between the sizes, shapes, colors, and the different ways that they grow. This is a great opportunity to show him the difference between ripe and unripe fruit. Make sure you explain that unripe berries will not ripen once picked so, if they are still green or white in places, then he should leave them on the plants. As he picks the fruit, you can examine it together; ask him if each one is ripe and how he can tell.

   It's only natural to pop the occasional strawberry into your mouth while picking but fruit should always be washed before eating, so try to keep his sampling to a minimum, or he will inevitably end up with stomachache.

   Make sure you don't pick a lot more fruit than you will use— explain to your child that fruit will become rotten if not used. You can use the fruit to make dishes together such as a fruit salad, or Fruit Kebabs (see page 22).

Strawberry smoothie

4
servings

Smoothies are a great way to get more nutrients into your child's diet. Both the strawberries and banana are good sources of fiber, which helps maintain a healthy digestive system. Plus, both strawberries and orange juice contain antioxidants, including vitamin C, that help preserve the immune system.

1. Help your child put the strawberries into a strainer and rinse them with cold water.

2. Use a small knife to cut the stems off the strawberries and cut each strawberry in half. Then let your child place the sliced berries into the blender.

3. Next, show her how to peel the banana, and, using a plastic knife, help her to cut the banana in half and place it in the blender.

4. She can then spoon the yogurt into the blender on top of the fruit, and add the orange juice and ice cubes.

5. Place the top on the blender and let your child turn it on until the mixture is smooth. Pour 1 cup of the smoothie into each of the tall glasses and serve with a straw.

Ingredients

1 cup fresh strawberries

1 medium banana

1 cup of 1% low-fat or fat-free plain yogurt

1 cup pulp-free orange juice

2 cups ice cubes

Equipment

A strainer

A small knife

A blender

A spoon

4 tall glasses

4 straws

Helpful hint

If you don't have fresh berries on hand (or they're out of season), use 2 cups of frozen strawberries instead. With frozen fruit you will not need to use ice cubes in the recipe.

When is fruit ripe to eat?

Most types of fruit have very clear visible indicators of their ripening stages (especially bananas), so they are a great way to demonstrate to children the difference between unripe, ripe, and overripe fruit, and which one is best to eat. They'll also start to learn what signs to look for, and how to apply that to other foods.

You will need

3–6 different types of fruit (including a banana), with 3 pieces of each: 1 underripe, 1 ripe and 1 overripe

1 chopping board and knife

Place all of the fruit out, in front of your child, explaining to him that fruit goes through different stages of ripeness, and that he needs to put the pieces in the correct order.

Starting with the bananas, ask him to put them in order starting with the unripe one. If he struggles to get the order right, give him clues for what to look for, such as the color, texture, firmness, or smell.

When they are in the right order, cut the banana open so that he can see inside, and compare how the flesh of each looks – offer him a little to taste of each, although he may refuse the overripe one!

Bananas show the stages of the ripening process very clearly, so it's a good one to start with to get him familiar with the signs to look out for with the rest of the pieces of fruit. Your child should start to find it easier to tell which pieces are ripe and which aren't.

Baked blueberry French toast

8 servings

This is an ideal breakfast—by prepping it the night before, you and your child will have time to make it together without the morning rush, have no cleanup in the morning, and everyone can enjoy it hot from the oven. Plus, using whole-wheat bread, half egg whites, and adding blueberries means you have a much more nutritional package than with regular French toast so your kids start their day on the right foot.

1. Ask your child to coat a baking pan with cooking spray and then set aside.

2. Slice the bread into ½-inch thick slices (you should end up with about 16 slices in total). Let your child arrange the slices in the baking pan, so that they are laid out flat in a single layer, with as little overlap as possible.

3. She can then pour the egg whites, whole eggs, milk, and vanilla into a medium bowl. Show her how to whisk the mixture together, using a fork or whisk, and then let her continue.

4. When the ingredients are well-combined, help her to pour the mixture evenly over the bread in the pan.

Ingredients

Nonstick cooking spray

1 loaf challah bread, preferably whole-wheat

4 large egg whites

4 large whole eggs

1 cup nonfat milk

1–2 tsp vanilla extract

2 tbsp brown sugar

Ground cinnamon, to taste

2 cups blueberries, fresh or frozen

Equipment

A 9 x 13-inch baking pan

A bread knife

A medium bowl

A fork or whisk

A strainer

Paper towels

Plastic wrap

5　Place the blueberries in the strainer, rinse, and pat dry with paper towel.

6　Let her sprinkle the brown sugar and cinnamon onto the bread in an even layer, followed by the blueberries.

7　Cover the pan with plastic wrap and refrigerate overnight.

8　In the morning, or whenever you wish to eat the French toast, preheat the oven to 350°F.

9　Remove the plastic wrap from the pan and place in the oven to bake for 40 minutes. It is ready when the bread is golden and slightly puffed.

Helpful hints

- If you don't have fresh berries or they're out of season, use unsweetened frozen berries instead. Frozen fruit is nutritionally comparable to fresh, and in off seasons it's even better because it hasn't been shipped from far away.

- Top the French toast with a dollop of nonfat plain or Greek yogurt and a drizzle of maple syrup for a protein boost and some added sweetness.

Grilled plums with yogurt dip

4 servings

Grilling fruit is a great way to make it more interesting. Plums are an excellent source of the antioxidants anthocyanins, which are commonly found in red and purple fruits and vegetables, and vitamin C.

1. Cut the plums in half by cutting along the seam to the pit, then show your child how to twist each half in opposite directions to separate them. Remove the pits.

2. Help him to lightly brush the plums with olive oil, using his fingers, and set them aside.

3. Spray the grill with cooking spray and heat it to medium-high. When it is hot, add the plums to the grill and cook for about 5 minutes. Flip the plums and cook on the other side for another 5 minutes.

4. While the plums are grilling, ask your child to add the yogurt and honey to a bowl and mix them together using a fork until they are well combined.

5. When the plums are finished cooking, remove them from the grill and set one plum on each plate. Help your child spoon approximately ¼-cup of the yogurt-honey dip on each plate (next to or on top of the plums—he can decide).

Ingredients

4 plums

Olive oil

Nonstick cooking spray

1 cup nonfat Greek or plain yogurt

4 tsp honey

Equipment

A knife

A grill or grill pan

A spatula

A small to medium bowl

A fork

4 plates

A spoon

Homemade applesauce

It's almost as easy to make fresh applesauce as it is to buy it in jars at the grocery store, and with this recipe you'll have a snack that's lower in sugar and higher in fiber. Each $\frac{1}{2}$-cup serving is equivalent to one serving of fruit. Apples also contain important phytochecmicals—these are good-for-you compounds found naturally in plants, which may protect the brain, heart, and arteries, and they are a rich source of fiber, thanks for the most part to the skin of the apple.

Ingredients

4 medium apples

$\frac{1}{2}$ cup water

$\frac{1}{4}$ cup brown sugar

1 tsp ground cinnamon

Equipment

An apple corer (optional)

A knife

A saucepan with lid

A bowl

A potato masher

1. Ask your child to rinse the apples in cold water.

2. Using an apple corer or knife, core the apples and chop them into quarters. Let your child place them in a saucepan, and then add the water, sugar, and cinnamon.

3. Cover and place the saucepan over medium heat. Cook for 20 minutes or until the apples are soft and mushy.

4. Turn off heat and transfer the apple mixture to a bowl. Help your child mash the apples with a potato masher. Add more cinnamon to taste if needed. Then cool and serve.

Which one's gone?

When you can turn learning into a fun game, you're much more likely to get your children interested. This fruit memory game is fun to play together, but your child will also be learning the names of different types of fruits, and having her memory tested. It can be played with as many or as few children as you want.

You will need

An assortment of fruit (no more than six pieces)

A tray

A small towel

First, tell your child that you're going to play the fruit memory game, and lay all of the fruit out on the tray. Make sure she is familiar with all of the names of the fruit—point at each one and ask her to tell you its name.

Cover the fruit with the small towel and then choose one piece of fruit, and remove it at the same time as the towel, so that your child can't see which one you've taken. Ask her to look at the remaining fruit and guess which one is gone.

If she struggles to remember, give her hints about the fruit, such as the shape and color, until she gets it right. Then you can replace the fruit, and start all over again, removing a different piece this time, and continue playing until you've used all of the fruit. And when she's become familiar with the more common types of fruit, you can start to introduce some more exotic varieties.

Colorful fruit kebabs

6 servings

These colorful fruit kebabs are a great way to introduce children to new fruits with flavors and textures they may not have had before. You can use any fruit available at the supermarket and your children's preferences. One skewer provides the equivalent of one serving of fruit.

① Help your child peel the banana, and then, using a plastic knife, slice it into ½-inch-thick round slices and place them in a bowl.

② Peel and cut the pineapple into chunks and let your child place them in a separate bowl.

③ Show him how to use the melon baller, and let him try if he is able, until you have 1 cup of watermelon balls, which he can place in a third bowl.

④ Then let him rinse off the grapes, blueberries, and strawberries, and place each fruit into a separate bowl.

⑤ Place each bowl of fruit in the center of a table or kitchen counter, and show your child how to make his skewers, adding on each piece of fruit in whatever order he likes.

Ingredients

1 medium banana

A pineapple

A watermelon

½ cup seedless grapes, green or red

½ cup blueberries or raspberries

6 medium strawberries

Equipment

A plastic knife

6 bowls

A sharp knife

A melon baller

6 wooden skewers

PB and banana cutouts

1 serving

Peanut butter is a great compliment to bananas, and a spread children love. This recipe has a serving of whole fruit and makes a nutritious and delicious sandwich your children will love to eat and make for themselves. They'll love the added fun of cutting their own sandwich into different shapes, too!

1 Ask your child to help you spread one tablespoon of peanut butter on to each slice of bread.

2 Show her how to peel the banana and with a plastic or dull knife, help her slice the banana into ½-inch-thick round slices.

3 She can then place the banana slices on top of one slice of bread, and put the other slice of bread on top to complete the sandwich.

4 Let your child use the cookie cutters to cut out the sandwich into different shapes.

Ingredients

2 tbsp peanut butter, preferably natural

2 slices 100% whole-wheat bread

½ small banana

Equipment

A plastic knife

Cookie cutters

Helpful hint

It is best to use natural peanut butter that contains only peanuts (and possibly salt). Most store-bought jars of peanut butter contain sugar and partially hydrogenated oils, which are unhealthy trans fats.

Fruit or vegetable?

When young children are introduced to the different food groups, it's not always clear to them how to tell which are fruit and which are vegetables. The best way to make it clear to them and really get them involved is with a practical demonstration, so that they can really see how to spot the differences between fruit and vegetables.

Start off by asking your child if he knows how to tell if something is a fruit. Most children will say that fruit is sweet, but you can tell him that although that is often true, it's not the whole story.

  Put the potato and tomato onto the chopping board first, and ask him if either of them are fruit. Then cut both of them open, and show him that the tomato has seeds and the potato doesn't. This, you can explain, is the key characteristic of a fruit—it has seeds because it is the reproductive organ of the plant or tree.

  Go through the rest of the fruit and vegetables you have selected, choosing two at a time. With each pair, ask your child if he can tell you which ones are fruit, and which are vegetables. Then cut them open, and let him see if he is right. Let him try a little of each one as well so that he can compare the flavors and sweetness of each.

A selection of fruit such as tomato, pumpkin, grapes, cucumber, a fruit with a pit, any citrus fruit, apple, strawberry, and a banana

A few vegetables such as a potato, carrot, and cabbage

A chopping board and knife

A tray large enough to put the fruit and vegetables on

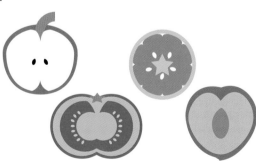

2 Vegetables

As many parents know, it can be difficult to convince children to eat their "greens." By focusing on the fun elements within these recipes such as stuffing, dipping, or even just using a more appealing name, you can engage your children's interest and they'll soon discover that fresh and seasonal vegetables aren't just good for them, but taste delicious too!

Sweet potato fries

4 servings

White potatoes can be part of a healthy, balanced diet for kids, but sweet potatoes are brimming with many more nutrients. They are a very good source of potassium, fiber, and vitamin C and beta-carotene, two antioxidants that help kids stay healthy.

1. Preheat the oven to 425°F. Ask your child to coat the baking pan with cooking spray and then set aside.

2. Slice the sweet potatoes lengthwise, making thin, long strips (you don't need to peel them first). Let your child place the potatoes in a medium bowl.

3. Help her to measure out the oil, salt, and spices (you may have to help steady her hands) and then pour and sprinkle these over the sweet potatoes.

4. Give her a spoon to toss the ingredients together (or she can use her hands), until the potatoes are coated with seasoning, and then place them onto the baking sheet and spread into a single layer.

5. Place the baking sheet in the oven and bake for about 30–40 minutes, turning the fries once, until they are lightly browned. Serve the fries with ketchup or honey-mustard dipping sauce (page 94), if desired.

Ingredients

Nonstick cooking spray

2 medium sweet potatoes

2 tbsp vegetable oil or peanut oil

¼ tsp salt

¼ tsp chili powder (optional)

¼ tsp cinnamon (optional)

Equipment

A baking sheet

A sharp knife

A cutting board

A medium-sized bowl

Measuring spoons

A large spoon

Roasted baby cabbages

Brussels sprouts have a bad reputation, but they are delicious and full of vitamins and minerals. They are part of the cruciferous family, which means they are a good source of fiber and antioxidants, and are rich in vitamins C and K, which help heal wounds and decrease inflammation—especially good for active kids! To make it appeal more to children, I like to call them baby cabbages—the cute factor is always a good trick.

Ingredients

Nonstick cooking spray

1 lb Brussels sprouts

1 tbsp olive oil

Salt and freshly ground black pepper

Equipment

A baking pan

A strainer

A paring knife

A cutting board

A medium-sized mixing bowl

1. Preheat the oven to 400°F. Let your child spray a baking pan with cooking spray and set aside.

2. Ask him to rinse the Brussels sprouts in a strainer under cold water.

3. Cut off the bottom of the sprouts and then let your child help remove the outer leaves.

4. Add the sprouts to the mixing bowl and ask your child to toss them with the olive oil, salt, and pepper. Then, let him spread them out in the baking pan.

5. Roast the vegetables uncovered for about 15–20 minutes. Serve hot.

Mashed squash

Mashed potatoes are a popular side dish that kids seem to love, but when they're filled with butter, cream, and whole milk, their nutritional value goes way down. Mashed squash is brimming with nutrients and the natural sweetness of the squash is intensified from being roasted. Kabocha squash is a type of winter squash that is a cross between butternut squash, sweet potato, and pumpkin. It is a very good source of beta-carotene, vitamin C, potassium, and fiber.

Ingredients

1 kabocha squash, about 3–4 lbs

1 tbsp olive oil

Salt and freshly ground pepper

Ground cinnamon

Equipment

A knife

A cutting board

A spoon

A baking sheet

A large bowl

A fork

1. Preheat the oven to 400°F.

2. Cut the squash in half and, using a spoon, have your child scoop out the seeds. Then she can rub olive oil on both halves.

3. Place the squash halves cut side down on the baking sheet and roast in the oven for 30–45 minutes, until the flesh is very soft. Remove from the oven and set aside to cool slightly until you are able to handle it.

4. Help your child spoon out the flesh of the squash and place in a large bowl. Using a fork, she can then mash the squash until it is smooth and there are no more large chunks. Add the salt, pepper, and cinnamon to taste and stir again to combine the flavors.

Growing seeds and vegetable tops

Growing your own vegetables is a great way to get children interested in the role that plants play in providing us with food and the care and nurturing required to help them grow. It will also introduce them to basic gardening skills and let them try out their green thumbs.

Explain to your child that he is going to do a growing experiment using seeds and vegetable tops. Help him to lightly dampen the blotting paper, and then fold it in half and into a circle to fit inside the jam jar, trimming off any excess. Repeat with the other jar. Then put a broad bean seed in each jar, between the glass and the paper, about halfway down the jar.

   When the jars are done, fill the saucers with a little water and place a vegetable top in each.

   Your child should keep an eye on the progress of the beans and vegetable tops over the next few days and ensure they don't dry out. He can also record the progress of the plants by making a diary, and taking pictures (or drawings) and measurements, to show what happens to each one, which parts start to grow, and how fast.

You will need

Some blotting paper, kitchen paper or coffee filter paper, to line the jars

Two tall jam jars with wide openings

A couple of broad bean seeds

A saucer for each vegetable top

A selection of root vegetable tops such as carrot, turnip, or beetroot

A notebook

A ruler

Roasted root vegetables

Roasting vegetables causes them to caramelize, which enhances their flavor, and adds a sweetness that is often lacking in vegetables. Root vegetables, such as carrots, parsnips, potatoes, turnips, and onions, are a staple come winter, because they can stand up to the cold weather.

1 Preheat the oven to 400°F. Spray a baking pan with cooking spray and set aside.

2 Give your child the carrots and parsnips to rinse in cold water.

3 Show her how to peel the vegetables, and then let her try, with your help. Cut each vegetable in half lengthwise and then crosswise into about six to eight chunks each. Place the vegetables in a medium to large mixing bowl.

4 Let your child add the olive oil, salt, rosemary, and pepper to the vegetables, and toss well to mix. Then have her spread the vegetables in the baking pan.

5 Roast the vegetables uncovered for about 10 minutes. Toss the vegetables and then return to the oven and reduce the temperature to 375°F. Roast for 15–20 minutes until the vegetables are soft (but not mushy).

Ingredients

Nonstick cooking spray

5 medium carrots
(about $2/3$ lb)

2 large parsnips
(about 1 lb)

1 tbsp olive oil

Salt and freshly
ground black pepper

Rosemary, fresh or
dried, to taste

Equipment

A baking pan

A vegetable peeler

A sharp knife

A cutting board

A medium or large
mixing bowl

Corn, tomato, and avocado salad

6 servings

This summery salad is the perfect light side dish to pair with your barbecue favorites. If your kids haven't yet tried avocado, there's no better time to start than with this recipe. Lots of kids love corn, but most people don't realize the nutritional value of this starchy vegetable. It's a good source of B vitamins, including folate and thiamin, vitamin C, and fiber. Tomatoes are also a good source of vitamin C, and avocados, which are technically fruit, are a terrific source of healthy monounsaturated fat and many vitamins and minerals, including vitamin E, magnesium, potassium, and even more vitamin C.

1. Help your child shuck the ears of corn. Place the corn in a pot of boiling water, and cook them for 2–3 minutes. Remove and set aside.

2. Spray a grill pan or outside grill with cooking spray. On a medium-high heat, grill the corn for 10 minutes, turning every few minutes until all of the sides have grill marks. Remove from grill and allow to cool.

3. Once it is cool enough to touch, use a paring knife to cut the kernels off the cob into a medium bowl. Be sure to cut very close to the cob to use as much corn as possible.

Ingredients

3 ears of corn

Nonstick cooking spray

1 cup grape tomatoes

1 avocado

2 tbsp extra-virgin olive oil

2 tbsp rice vinegar

Salt and freshly ground pepper

Handful of fresh basil leaves

Equipment

A large pot

Grill or grill pan

A paring knife

A medium bowl

A plastic or dull knife

Measuring spoons

A small bowl

A whisk or fork

4. Halve the tomatoes and let your child add them to the bowl.

5. Slice the avocado in half and remove the pit. Help your child scoop out the flesh, and then dice into medium-sized pieces, using a plastic knife. Add the avocado to the corn and tomato mixture.

6. Your child can then measure out the olive oil and vinegar into a small bowl, and add salt and pepper, and then whisk well to combine. Add to the salad and toss to mix.

7. Ask your child to rinse the basil leaves and tear them into pieces. Before serving, he can add the basil and toss the salad once more.

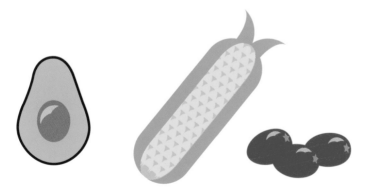

Cole slaw

Cole slaw is usually full of mayonnaise, which means lots of calories and saturated fat. This version is lightened up by using vinegar and oil as the dressing, but it still has a wonderful flavor. Cabbage is a cruciferous vegetable in the same family as kale, Brussels sprouts, and broccoli. It is an excellent source of vitamins K and C, and darker varieties are also a good source of antioxidants beta-carotene and quercetin. Cabbage is also low in calories, with only 17 per cup.

1. Slice and shred the cabbage, slice the onion into half moons and peel the carrots and cut into thin strips. Have your child combine the sliced vegetables in a large bowl.

2. Then help her to measure out the rice vinegar, olive oil, and sugar, and add to a small bowl with salt and pepper. She can then whisk the ingredients together and drizzle the dressing over the vegetables, making sure to coat them completely.

3. Refrigerate for at least 20 minutes to allow flavors to marinate before serving.

Ingredients

$\frac{1}{2}$ head green cabbage

1 red onion

2 carrots

2 tbsp rice vinegar

2 tbsp extra-virgin olive oil

1 tbsp sugar

Salt and freshly ground black pepper

Equipment

A sharp knife

A cutting board

A peeler

A large bowl

Measuring spoons

A small bowl

A whisk or fork

Over ground or under ground?

There are so many different types of vegetables, it can be a lot for children to take in. One easy way to help them understand the different varieties, and how to tell them apart, is by exploring where and how they grow.

Tell your child that he's going to find out how different vegetables can grow, both over and under ground. First, let him make the background—with the paper in a landscape position, ask him to color in the paper, making the top half blue and the bottom half brown.

   Go through the pictures together, and let him choose a vegetable with which he is familiar. Hold up the picture, and ask him if she can guess where the vegetable grows. He may need some guidance and clues the first time you play this game. If he doesn't guess correctly, tell him the right answer and explain how it grows, and how you can tell. Then ask him to stick it on the paper, either in the blue or the brown half, depending whether it grows over or under ground.

   Then go back to the magazines, to find some more pictures, and let him try to guess those as well. Keep going until the paper is full. As he becomes more confident, you can make this more advanced by choosing vegetables for him with which he is less familiar.

You will need

A large sheet of paper, preferably A3-sized

Some colored pencils (or felt-tipped pens, crayons, or paints)

Pictures of different vegetables, for example, carrots, potatos, onions, broad beans, bell peppers, broccoli

A glue stick

A pair of scissors

Stuffed butternut squash

4 servings

This hearty, veggie filled dish looks beautiful on the table, and is as fun to prepare as it is to eat. You can stuff the squash with any grain (such as brown rice or barley). This recipe uses the Quinoa Salad recipe from page 76.

1. Preheat oven to 350°F.

2. Slice the squash in half. Give your child a spoon so that she can scoop out all of the seeds.

3. Let her combine the oil, salt, and pepper in a small bowl and rub the mixture on the flesh of the squash.

4. Place the squash in a shallow baking pan, flesh side down, with 1 inch of water, and roast for 45 minutes, or until the flesh is soft and tender.

5. Remove the squash from the oven and show your child how to fill the squash cavities with about 2 cups of the Quinoa Salad. She can then sprinkle the Parmesan cheese on top of each squash if desired.

6. Place the stuffed squash halves back in the baking pan and bake for another 10 minutes.

Ingredients

1 butternut squash

2 tsp olive oil

Salt and freshly ground black pepper

4 cups Quinoa Salad

¼ cup grated Parmesan cheese (optional)

Equipment

A sharp knife

A cutting board

A spoon

A small bowl

A baking pan

Helpful hint

If available, you can replace the butternut squash with two acorn squash—the smaller size of these appeal to children, and make a smaller portion.

Spaghetti squash and cheesy sauce

4–6 servings

Using spaghetti squash in place of regular spaghetti is a fun way to get your kids excited about eating vegetables—plus they'll love getting in the kitchen to help remove the "noodles" from the cooked squash! Spaghetti squash has less than a quarter of the calories of traditional spaghetti and is filled with important nutrients like beta-carotene and vitamin C, antioxidants that help increase immunity and promote vision and healthy skin.

1. Preheat the oven to 350°F.

2. Ask your child to rinse the squash, and then pierce a few holes in it with a fork.

3. Place the whole squash onto a baking sheet and bake for 45–60 minutes, or until the skin is soft (check by pressing on the squash with an oven mitt) and the inside is tender.

4. While the squash is baking, prepare the tomato sauce. If he is able, let your child open the cans of beans and tomatoes, using a can opener. He can then rinse the beans, and set half a cup of them aside.

5. Peel and mince the garlic cloves and peel and dice the onion. Then sauté both in a medium-sized skillet in the oil until they are soft and slightly browned (about 4–5 minutes).

Ingredients

1 medium spaghetti squash

1 (16-oz) can low-sodium cannellini beans (optional)

1 (28-oz) can low-sodium crushed tomatoes

2 garlic cloves

1 medium white onion

2 tsp olive oil

1 tsp dried basil

1/2 tsp dried oregano

Salt and freshly ground black pepper

1/2 cup shredded mozzarella cheese

2 tbsp grated Parmesan cheese

6 Carefully help your child pour the tomatoes and beans into the skillet with the garlic and onion. Then he can add the basil, oregano, and a pinch of salt and pepper. Simmer for 15 minutes.

7 During the last few minutes of simmering, help your child add half of the mozzarella to the sauce, then stir gently. Turn off the heat and pour the tomato sauce from the pot into a serving bowl.

8 Remove the squash from the oven, and allow to cool for 10–15 minutes, then cut it in half lengthwise.

9 Give your child a large spoon to scoop out the seeds, and discard them. Then show him how to carefully take a fork and scrape out the "noodles" a little at a time. The flesh inside the squash will separate into spaghetti-like strands. Make sure that all of the flesh from the center to the outside is scraped, being careful not to include any stray seeds.

10 Place one cup of spaghetti squash "noodles" on each plate, and help your child spoon about half a cup of tomato sauce onto each serving. Let him sprinkle the remaining mozzarella cheese and Parmesan cheese evenly among plates of the "spaghetti" and sauce. Serve immediately.

Equipment

A fork

A baking sheet

Oven mitts

A can opener

A strainer

A cutting board

A sharp knife

A medium-sized skillet

A spatula

A serving bowl

A large spoon

A fork

Exploring flavor

Young children are still developing their sense of taste, and learning how to identify flavors. In this activity, your child will explore the difference between sweet, sour, and salty tastes.

Slice the food into bite-sized pieces, and place them all on the large plate, setting the three dishes in front of you and your child. Tell her that she is going to explore her sense of taste, by trying a little of the different foods in front of her, and saying if it tastes salty, sour, or sweet, without seeing what the food is.

Help him to put on the blindfold, and select a food for him to try. Tell her that if it tastes salty, she should place it on the dish on the left; if it tastes sour, it should go in the middle; and sweet food should go on the right.

Let her taste the food and place it on which dish she thinks it should go on. Get her familiar with the words, by asking her to say, "This tastes salty (or sour or sweet)," as she places each one on a dish. Continue until all the different foods have been tasted.

Once she has the hang of this, you can extend the activity by introducing different foods and tastes into the game.

You will need

3 foods, one each that is sweet, sour, or salty (for example, an apple, a lemon, and salty potato chips)

1 large plate

3 small dishes

Paper towels

A blindfold

Sticks and dip

Kids enjoy the activity of dipping food, so even the pickiest eaters will love vegetable sticks when you serve them with dip. You can use any crisp and crunchy vegetables you like, and you can serve this with the simple dips below, or the Cucumber Yogurt Dip (see page 57) or the White Bean Dip (see page 45).

1. Give your child the cucumber and pepper to rinse in cold water.

2. Help him peel the cucumber and cut it into sticks using a dull or plastic knife, and then cut the pepper into sticks as well.

3. Once all of the vegetables are prepared, he can arrange them on a plate.

4. For a simple dip, ask your child to place the cream cheese into a bowl, then add the tomato ketchup and mix until combined. Or for alternative options, try the White Bean Dip on the opposite page or turn to page 57 for a Cucumber Yogurt Dip. Serve your dip of choice with the vegetables.

Ingredients

1 medium cucumber

1 medium red or yellow bell pepper

1 cup baby carrots

$2/3$ cup mayonnaise

$1/3$ cup tomato ketchup

Equipment

A peeler

A cutting board

A dull or plastic knife, or scissors

A medium to large plate

A small bowl

A spoon

White bean dip

8–10 servings

This is a wholesome dip, as white beans are a great source of fiber, protein, folate, magnesium, and potassium. You can serve the white bean dip with sliced vegetables (see opposite page) or pita chips (see page 69).

1. Help your child open the cans of beans. Then she can pour the beans into a strainer to rinse them, and then pour them into the food processor (or blender).

2. Peel and mince the garlic and ask your child to add it to the beans. She can also add the olive oil, salt, pepper, and rosemary.

3. Cut the lemon in half and put one half in a hand juicer, showing her how to squeeze the juice out. Let her juice the other half, and then help her to measure out 3 tablespoons of juice and add to the bean mixture.

4. Cover the food processor and let your child turn it on for about 10–15 seconds. Then remove the cover and, using a spatula, show her how to mix the ingredients together, and scrape the sides of the bowl.

5. Cover the processor again and let your child turn it on for another 10–15 seconds until the mixture is smooth. Then pour into a serving bowl.

Ingredients

2 (15-oz) cans of white beans, such as cannellini or butter beans

2 garlic cloves

3 tbsp olive oil

Salt and freshly ground black pepper

Rosemary, fresh or dried, to taste

1 lemon

Equipment

A can opener

A strainer

A food processor or blender

A cutting board

A knife

A hand juicer

A spatula

A serving bowl

Edamame salad

6–8 servings

Edamame has become increasingly popular over the years, especially with kids. They are green soybeans that grow inside an inedible pod. When served in these pods, you have a fun, nutrient-rich snack for your kids. They are a very good source of vegetarian protein, fiber, and healthy omega-3 fats.

1. Cook the edamame according to the package directions. Drain and transfer to a medium bowl. Set aside to cool for about 10 minutes.

2. Chop the pepper and scallions, and help your child to grate the carrot (you should end up with about half a cup of grated carrot). Ask him to add the vegetables to the edamame beans.

3. In a small mixing bowl, your child can add and then whisk together the sesame oil, rice vinegar, and soy sauce to make the dressing.

4. Pour the dressing over the edamame salad and toss to combine. Season with salt and pepper.

Ingredients

1 (14-oz) bag of shelled edamame, frozen

1 large red bell pepper

3 scallions

1 carrot

2 tbsp sesame oil

1 tbsp rice vinegar

2 tsp low-sodium soy sauce

Freshly ground black pepper

Equipment

A strainer

A small to medium pot

A medium bowl

A cutting board

A grater

A small mixing bowl

A whisk or fork

Vegetables around the world

These days our children have the opportunity to try vegetables from around the world throughout the year. With the help of a map of the world, they can start to grasp where different vegetables come from, as well as teaching them a little about the quality of locally sourced seasonal produce.

Gather a selection of exotic vegetables from different parts of the world, as well as some locally grown produce, and place them on the tray with the map or globe.

Start with the exotic vegetables. Give each one to your child, and see if she can identify it (you may need to tell her if she is unfamiliar with it) and if she knows where it grows.

Then look on the packaging for the country of origin and help her locate it on the map. Show her how far it has to travel to get to your region, and compare this to the local vegetables. You can explain that the exotic vegetables need to be grown in that part of the world because of the different climates.

Then cook each vegetable (if necessary) and both of you taste a little of each one. Compare the taste of the exotic vegetables compared to the local vegetables, and see if you can tell a difference in taste. Explain that local vegetables haven't had to travel as far to get here, which means that they are much fresher, healthier, and tastier.

You will need

A selection of both exotic and local vegetables

A map of the world or a globe

A tray

A chopping board and a knife

Tomato soup

This simple, healthy, homemade tomato soup is a great way to help your kids eat more vegetables. Tomatoes contain many beneficial vitamins and minerals, such as potassium, fiber, and vitamins A and C. Cooked tomatoes are an especially rich source of lycopene, a powerful disease-fighting antioxidant. This soup has no added sugar and very little added fat. Make the meal complete with a Grilled Cheese Sandwich (see page 64).

1. Chop the onion, celery, and carrot, then add the olive oil to a large pot and sauté the vegetables over a medium heat, helping your child stir them until they are soft. Mince the garlic and let your child add it to the pot. Cook for another minute.

2. Once the vegetables are soft and coated in olive oil, let your child open and add the contents of the can of diced tomatoes, as well as the broth and basil. Again, let him carefully stir the mixture. Bring to a boil, then reduce the heat and simmer for 30 minutes.

3. Remove from heat. Use an immersion blender to blend until smooth (or blend small batches in a food processor or regular blender and then return to the pot). Season with the salt and pepper, and serve. For a creamier texture, stir in one cup of nonfat milk.

Ingredients

1 medium onion

3 celery stalks

1 large carrot

1 tbsp olive oil

1 garlic clove

1 (28-oz) can diced tomatoes

4 cups low-sodium vegetable or chicken broth

1 tsp dried basil

$1/4$ tsp salt

$1/4$ tsp black pepper

1 cup nonfat milk (optional)

Equipment

A sharp knife

A cutting board

A large pot

Measuring spoons

A can opener

Stirring spoons

An immersion blender or food processor

3 Dairy and eggs

Both eggs and dairy products are easy to make into plenty of child-friendly dishes, perfect for meals and for quick snacks. And they provide plenty of nutrients that growing children need, such as protein, calcium, and vitamins A and B_{12}. However, dairy can be high in saturated fat, so where possible, choose skimmed or low-fat options.

Egg wrap

2 servings

Change up the typical egg sandwich by serving it in a tortilla wrap! Scramble the eggs, toss in some veggies, add some cheese, and you have a great meal for any time of day. You can also get creative with the recipe by adding other vegetables or toppings to the wrap, such as mushrooms, peppers, zucchini, turkey bacon, or avocado—whatever your child likes to eat.

1. Chop the onion and then heat the oil in a small or medium skillet over a medium–high heat.

2. When the oil is hot, add the onions and sauté for 1–2 minutes. Add the broccoli and continue sautéing until the florets are soft, but not mushy. Turn off the heat and transfer the cooked vegetables to a bowl.

3. In a small mixing bowl, help your child add together the egg, egg whites, milk, thyme, salt, and pepper, and then whisk until the ingredients are combined.

4. Coat the skillet with nonstick cooking spray and heat over medium–high. When it is hot, add the egg mixture. As the eggs begin to set, show your child how to scramble them with a spatula.

Ingredients

1 tbsp olive oil

½ medium onion

½ cup broccoli florets

1 large egg

2 large egg whites

¼ cup nonfat or 1% milk

¼ tsp dried thyme

Salt and freshly ground black pepper

Nonstick cooking spray

1 (8-inch) whole-wheat tortilla

½ cup shredded reduced-fat (2%) cheddar cheese

5 Once the eggs are scrambled and mostly cooked, add the vegetables back to the pan, and mix them all together until eggs are fully cooked. Turn off the heat and let the mixture rest.

6 Have your child place the tortilla on a plate. He can then sprinkle the cheese along the center of the tortilla, and place the egg and vegetable mixture on top.

7 Help him roll the tortilla to form a wrap, and place two toothpicks in the wrap on the side that is folded over, about 2 inches from the ends. Slice the wrap in half and place each half on a plate.

A small to medium skillet

A sharp knife

A cutting board

A bowl

A small mixing bowl

A whisk

A spatula

Toothpicks

2 plates

Egg-in-a-hole

1 serving

Here is a protein-packed, grain-filled breakfast that is simple and quick. The egg white provides protein, but the yolk is where the majority of nutrients lie, including choline, which plays a key role in brain development; folate, which helps produce and maintain new cells; and vitamin D, which helps absorb calcium.

Ingredients

1 slice whole-wheat bread

Nonstick cooking spray

1 egg

Salt and freshly ground black pepper

Equipment

A glass or plastic cup

A griddle or pan

A spatula

1. Give your child the glass or plastic cup and press into the center of the bread to cut a circle; remove the circle and reserve.

2. Spray a griddle or pan with cooking spray (you can also use olive oil or butter) and place the bread on the hot griddle. After 2–3 minutes, flip the toast over.

3. Show your child how you crack an egg into a cup, and then pour it into the "hole" in the bread. If you're cooking more than one, let her try the next one.

4. Cook on medium heat until the egg is cooked as desired. Place the circle on the hot griddle as well, and cook until browned on both sides.

5. Serve the egg-in-a-hole with the crispy bread circle, which can be eaten on its own, or can be used to dip into the egg yolk.

Helpful hint

You can flip the egg-in-a-hole midway through cooking if your child likes her egg sunny-side down. Older children may be able to flip the egg with your help.

Caprese sticks

Take the traditional Caprese salad and make it a kid-favorite by letting them make their own skewers. During the summer, when tomatoes are at their peak, make these skewers using a colorful variety of cherry tomatoes.

1. Have your child rinse the basil leaves well, making sure to get rid of any grit, and dry them in a salad spinner.

2. Next, he can rinse the grape tomatoes and then pat them dry.

3. With a plastic or dull knife, show him how to cut each mozzarella ball in half, then let him try to do the rest.

4. Then, show him how to carefully slide one tomato onto a skewer, followed by half a mozzarella ball, and one basil leaf. Place the completed skewer on a platter and let him continue making the rest of the skewers.

5. When all of the skewers are done, drizzle them with olive oil and aged balsamic vinegar. Season with salt and pepper and serve immediately.

Ingredients

1 small bunch fresh basil

12 grape or cherry tomatoes

6 bocconcini or ciliegine (small mozzarella balls)

2 tbsp extra-virgin olive oil

1 tbsp aged balsamic vinegar

Salt and freshly ground black pepper

Equipment

A salad spinner

A small bowl

A plastic or dull knife

A cutting board

12 wooden skewers

A platter

Cucumber yogurt dip

This dip is perfect paired with vegetables (see Sticks and Dip page 44) or Pita Chips (see page 69). Greek yogurt is a great replacement for some other typical dip bases like mayonnaise and sour cream. It's packed with protein and calcium—a nutrient every child needs to grow strong bones! Just be sure to use nonfat yogurt to avoid the less healthy saturated fat.

1. Show your child how to peel the cucumber, halve lengthwise and remove the seeds. Then let help her grate the halves (or chop them up in a food processor) until coarse, but not mushy.

2. Show her how to drain the liquid from the grated cucumber by placing it in a strainer and covering it with a paper towel to squeeze out the excess juice. You may need to change the paper towel a few times.

3. In a medium bowl, have your child combine the yogurt, chives, garlic, lemon juice, and olive oil. Let her fold in the drained cucumber and season with salt and pepper. Add a sprinkle of cumin to taste.

4. Refrigerate until chilled and thickened (about an hour). Drain off excess liquid if there is any, and serve.

Ingredients

1 English cucumber

1 ½ cups nonfat Greek yogurt

2 tbsp chopped fresh chives

1–2 garlic cloves, minced

1 tbsp freshly squeezed lemon juice

1 tbsp extra-virgin olive oil

Salt and freshly ground pepper

Ground cumin, to taste

Equipment

A vegetable peeler

A knife

A cutting board

A grater or food processor

A strainer

Paper towels

A medium bowl

A spoon

Who laid the egg?

Most children love eggs, but they may not know where they come from, or that there are lots of types of egg laid by different birds. In this pairing game, children will learn that there are different eggs laid by different birds, and they'll also have a chance to test their memories, and find out which eggs are edible and which ones aren't.

You will need

Pictures of each type of bird to match the egg selection (below)

A selection of different readily-available eggs (such as chicken, duck, and quail)

Pictures of other eggs such as ostrich or distinctive garden bird eggs

Go through all of the different birds that you have selected to make sure that your child is familiar with their names.

Then, lay out all the eggs, including any pictures, in one row, and the pictures of the birds below. Make sure the eggs are placed on a surface that they can't roll off. Show your child that eggs need to be handled with care because of their fragile shell.

Tell your child that this is a matching game, and he needs to help each of the birds find their egg, by moving the picture of the bird above the egg it belongs with. If he is struggling to match them correctly, give him hints about the size of the egg and the size of the bird.

Once they are correctly matched, you can explain that the eggs we eat aren't fertilized, and that's why they aren't chicks. See if he can identify the birds whose eggs we commonly eat, and those we don't.

Cheesy egg muffin

6 servings

Who says muffins have to be sweet? These savory egg muffins are the perfect protein-filled breakfast for a weekend day. You can also make them in advance, to have later in the week as a midweek breakfast treat.

1. Preheat the oven to 350°F.

2. Give your child the muffin liners and ask her to put one in each slot of the muffin tin. Spray the liners with cooking spray, making sure to coat the sides and bottom well. Set aside.

3. Dice the mushrooms, and, if using, also chop the chives and dice the bacon.

4. In a medium mixing bowl, help your child combine the eggs, egg whites, mushrooms, cheese, and chives and bacon if using. Season with salt, pepper, and thyme. Get her to whisk mixture until it is blended.

5. Pour a third of a cup of the egg mixture into each of the muffin cups (they should be about two-thirds full).

6. Bake for 25–30 minutes, or until the muffins have risen and are slightly brown and set.

Ingredients

Nonstick cooking spray

1 cup mushrooms

3 chives (optional)

6 oz Canadian bacon (optional)

6 large whole eggs

6 large egg whites

1 cup grated Cheddar cheese, preferably reduced fat

1/4 tsp salt

Freshly ground black pepper

1/4 tsp dried thyme

Equipment

Muffin liners

A 6-hole muffin tin

A medium mixing bowl

A whisk or fork

Egg salad

2 servings

Kids are big fans of eggs, but when it comes to egg salad it's not always the best choice for their health. Traditional egg salad is filled with tablespoons of mayonnaise, which isn't so good for your little one's heart. This recipe cuts down on the saturated fat and cholesterol by using a combination of whole eggs and egg whites.

1 Let your child chop up the boiled eggs and the avocado flesh using a plastic knife, while you chop up the onion.

2 Have her place the eggs, avocado, and onion in a medium bowl, and then add the mustard and mayonnaise. Using a fork, ask her to mash the ingredients together. Season with salt and pepper.

3 Serve on whole-wheat bread, whole grain crackers, or by itself!

Ingredients

2 large hard boiled eggs

2 large hard boiled egg whites

½ avocado

¼ red onion

2 tsp Dijon mustard

1 tsp reduced-fat mayonnaise

Salt and freshly ground black pepper

Whole-wheat bread or whole grain crackers to serve

Equipment

A plastic or blunt knife

A cutting board

A sharp knife

A medium bowl

A fork

Yogurt parfait

1 serving

Kids love to assemble their own dishes and see their own creations! Help them make their own layered parfait for a wonderful visual treat as well as a nutrient-packed breakfast.

1. Let your child rinse the berries in a strainer and then place in a bowl. Ask him to place the yogurt and granola into separate bowls as well.

2. Help him put about a third of the yogurt in the bottom of the serving glass.

3. He can then layer a third of the berries and a third of the granola on top of the yogurt, and then repeat the layers with the remaining ingredients two more times.

4. Top with a drizzle of honey and serve.

Ingredients

¼ cup fresh berries

4 oz nonfat or 1% yogurt (plain, flavored, or use different ones for each layer)

¼ cup granola (see page 68)

Honey

Equipment

A strainer

3 bowls

A short, clear glass (8–10 oz in volume)

A spoon

Grilled cheese

Grilled cheese was one of my favorite lunches growing up, and what kid doesn't like the ooey, gooey, deliciousness of melted cheese and buttery toasted bread?

1. Ask your child to put the cheese slices between two slices of whole-wheat bread.

2. Melt the butter spread in a small skillet. Add the cheese sandwich and cook for about 2 minutes on the first side.

3. Show your child how to flip the sandwich and then cook for another 2 minutes. Flip a couple more times—older children may be able to flip the sandwich themselves, so if your child is able, let her try to flip it herself, with your help.

4. When the bread is toasted and the cheese is melted, remove the skillet from the heat, and transfer the sandwich to a plate. Serve hot.

Ingredients

2–3 slices reduced-fat Swiss or American cheese

2 slices whole-wheat bread

1 tsp trans-fat free light butter spread

Equipment

A small skillet

A spatula

A plate

A milk taste test

Milk is a great source of many vitamins and minerals that growing children need, especially calcium, and it's something that most kids enjoy. There are lots of different types of milk though, and this is a fun way for kids to explore the different flavors and where they come from.

You can start off by asking your child if he knows where milk comes from. He'll probably say from cows (if not, give him a few clues), and you can then tell him that's right, but there are lots of different types. You can explain that we can drink the milk of different animals as well, and that there are non-dairy options for people who are allergic to milk.

Pour a little of each different milk into a small cup (only use small quantities in this game—although milk is considered good for children, they shouldn't have too much, so don't exceed recommended daily limits), and write down the name of each one on a piece of paper, or you could draw a picture that corresponds to each one, and place each label with the correct glass. Both of you try a little of each milk and talk about the different flavor, and which ones you like the best.

Then ask her to close her eyes while you remove the labels and swap the order of the glasses. Ask her to try a little of each one again, and see if her favorite milk is still the same one, and if she can match up the labels with the correct glass of milk.

You will need

A variety of 3–6 different milks, such as full-fat, skimmed, goat, soy, rice and almond

A glass for each variety

A paper label for each variety

4 Bread, pasta, and grains

Bread, pasta, and grains provide complex carbohydrates—an important source of energy. Children are often drawn to the products made from white flour—try to introduce them to the whole-wheat varieties where possible as they are a much healthier option, with more vitamins, minerals, and fiber.

Cranberry pecan granola

22 servings

Granola sounds like a super healthy food, but you do need to watch the portion size. The combination of oats, nuts, dried fruit, and honey means a little bit goes a long way.

1. Preheat the oven to 350°F. Help your child to line a baking sheet with parchment paper, coat with cooking spray, and set aside.

2. In a large bowl, have her mix together the oats, pecans, cinnamon, and salt. Then, she can whisk the syrup or honey and oil in a measuring cup.

3. Next, help her pour the syrup mixture over the oat mixture and combine well, and then spread the mixture in a thin layer onto the prepared baking sheet.

4. Bake for 30 minutes, checking on it every 10 minutes and shaking the granola to make sure it all browns evenly.

5. When the granola is golden brown, remove from the oven and let cool for about 10 minutes. Transfer to a bowl or airtight container. Break up large chunks into smaller pieces, and toss in the dried cranberries.

Ingredients

Nonstick cooking spray

4 cups rolled oats

1 cup chopped pecans

1 1/2 tsp cinnamon

1/4 tsp salt

1/3 cup maple syrup or honey

2 tbsp vegetable oil

1 cup dried cranberries

Equipment

A baking sheet

Parchment paper

A large bowl

A measuring cup

A wooden spoon

A whisk or fork

An airtight container

Helpful hint

You can store the granola in an airtight container for up to 2 weeks.

Rosemary pita chips

12 servings

Pita chips serve as a great vehicle for picking up dips. Your kids will love these crispy chips no matter what you serve with them. Rosemary is an herb commonly used in Mediterranean cooking, and like other herbs, it adds a wonderful flavor to food without the addition of sodium.

1. Preheat the oven to 375°F.

2. Using a plastic knife, have your child cut the pita breads in half and then cut each half into 4 wedges, for a total of 8 wedges per pita.

3. Help him to measure out the oil and seasonings, pour them into a small bowl, and stir to combine.

4. Using his hands, he can then spread the oil mixture on both sides of the pita wedges.

5. Spread the wedges in a single layer on two baking sheets. Bake for about 5 minutes, then flip over and bake another 5 minutes, until the pitas are brown and crisp.

6. Remove from the oven and let cool completely before serving on their own or with a selection of dips. They can be stored in an airtight container for about a week.

Ingredients

6 (6½-inch) whole-wheat pita breads

6 tbsp olive oil

½ tsp salt

½ tsp freshly ground black pepper

2 tsp fresh rosemary, or 1 tsp dried

Equipment

A plastic knife

Measuring spoons

A small bowl

A fork

2 baking sheets

Make your own pizza

Kids and adults alike love pizza, and using whole-wheat dough provides the added benefit of fiber and nutrients.

1. Preheat oven to 425°F. Help your child brush or rub olive oil on a large baking sheet or pizza pan.

2. Chop the onion and pepper, and slice the mushrooms. Heat 1 tablespoon of oil in a skillet over medium heat. Add the onions and peppers and sauté for about 5 minutes, and then add the mushrooms and cook for another 1–2 minutes. Season vegetables with salt and pepper. Remove from the heat and set aside.

3. Lightly dust a work surface with flour. Using a rolling pin, help your child spread each ball of dough into a 6-inch circle, with a thicker border for the crust.

4. Transfer the pizza dough to the prepared baking sheet. Brush the dough with oil and bake for about 5 minutes.

5. Help your child spoon half of the tomato sauce over each pizza, and then add equal amounts of the vegetables, and mozzarella and Parmesan.

6. Bake the pizzas for 10–12 minutes, until the crust is golden brown. Remove from oven and top with a sprinkle of herbs and spices if using.

Ingredients

Olive oil

1 small onion

¼ medium red pepper

¼ medium yellow pepper

1 cup mushrooms

Salt and black pepper

Flour, for dusting

1 lb prepared whole-wheat pizza dough, cut in half

1 ½ cups canned tomato sauce

2 cups shredded part-skim mozzarella cheese

¼ cup shredded Parmesan cheese

Oregano and basil, dried or fresh (optional)

Red chili flakes (optional)

Equipment

A baking sheet

A paring knife

A cutting board

A medium skillet

A spatula

A rolling pin

A spoon

Very berry oatmeal

Stick-to-your-ribs oatmeal is a great way to start the morning any time of year, although especially in the winter. Oatmeal is a whole grain that is a great source of soluble fiber, which keeps you satisfied and full. It is also a great source of B vitamins, which are important for maintaining energy—something kids need a lot of! If fresh berries are out of season, you can use frozen ones instead.

Ingredients

1 cup whole strawberries

2 tbsp granulated sugar

1 tbsp lemon juice

2 tsp cornstarch

1 3/4 cup nonfat milk

1 cup rolled oats (not instant)

Equipment

A plastic or dull knife

A cutting board

2 small saucepans

Wooden spoons or spatulas

2 bowls

1. Show your child how to dice the strawberries, and then she can combine the strawberries, sugar, lemon juice, and cornstarch in a small saucepan.

2. Bring to a boil and stir constantly for about 3 minutes over a high heat, until the strawberries are mushy and thick. Cover and remove from the heat.

3. Your child can then pour the milk into another small saucepan. Bring to a boil, add the oats, and cook, letting her stir occasionally, over a medium heat for about 1–2 minutes (depending on the consistency you desire).

4. Divide the oatmeal between two bowls and top each with about half of the berry sauce. Serve hot.

Happy face waffles

How often do your kids get to play with their food? With this recipe they can play with their food, making any design they like. Peanut butter is a nutritious and delicious spread. It is an excellent source of good-for-you monounsaturated fat and vegetarian protein. It's also rich in vitamin E, an important nutrient that keeps your eyes, skin, and blood cells healthy. However, peanut butter is very high in calories, so stick to small portion sizes! It is best to use natural peanut butter with only peanuts (and possibly salt) in the ingredients.

Ingredients

2 whole grain waffles

2 tbsp natural peanut butter

1 cup blueberries

Equipment

A toaster

A plastic knife

A strainer

1. Toast the waffles in a toaster oven.

2. Ask your child to spread 1 tablespoon of peanut butter on each waffle.

3. Let him rinse the berries in the strainer and pat dry. Then he can "decorate" the peanut butter waffle with blueberries. He can make a smiley face or any other design he likes. You can also use a combination of different types of fruit, such as slices of banana, or strawberries.

Grow your own sandwich fillings

Being able to eat food that you have grown yourself is an exciting accomplishment. For young children with short attention spans though, it can be hard to keep their interest engaged in planting projects that take a while to grow. That's why cress and mustard seed planting is a great activity for your children, as they'll be able to see the results in just a few days.

Show your child the cress and mustard seeds, and tell her that she is going to grow them into plants that she will then be able to eat.

Place the paper towels on top of each other, and onto the tray. Let her dampen the sheets with the spray or sponge, but make sure she doesn't make the paper too wet. Then she can sprinkle the seeds over the top.

The seeds should take just a few days before they are fully grown. Make sure your child keeps an eye on them so that she can watch their progress as they grow, and keep the paper moist—if it looks dry, she can just respray it.

When the seeds are fully grown, you can add them to a filling such as egg mayonnaise, for a tasty sandwich.

To increase the fun for young children, you can also grow the seeds in empty egg shells. Fill the shells with moist paper to the top of the shell and plant in the same way. When grown, use a pen to add a face to the shell so that the cress becomes the "hair."

You will need

A packet of cress or mustard seeds

2 sheets paper towels

A small tray or the lid of a plastic container

1 plant spray or a wet sponge

Peanut noodles

4–6 servings

Soba is a thin noodle made from buckwheat flour. Buckwheat is actually a fruit seed, not a grain, which means it is safe to eat if you have a gluten or wheat intolerance (although you should check the labels on the package as not all are gluten-free). It is higher in fiber than white pasta, which means it is more satiating, and it has more nutrients.

1. Bring a large pot of unsalted water to a boil. Add the soba noodles and cook, stirring occasionally, until tender. Drain, rinse, and transfer them to a large bowl.

2. Mince the garlic, and let your child help you grate the ginger and juice the lime. Then let her add these to the food processor, along with the peanut butter, ¼ cup hot water, soy sauce, vinegar, chili paste, and brown sugar.

3. Process the ingredients until sauce is smooth, adding some more hot water if needed.

4. Chop and seed the cucumber, and chop the pepper and scallions. Let your child add the vegetables and the peanut sauce to the noodles. Toss to combine well, and serve.

Ingredients

½ lb soba noodles

1–2 garlic cloves

1-inch piece of fresh ginger

1 lime

⅓ cup natural peanut butter

2 tbsp low-sodium soy sauce

2 tbsp rice vinegar

1 tsp red chili paste

1 tbsp brown sugar

4 oz cucumber

1 large red bell pepper

1–2 oz scallions

Equipment

A large pot

A wooden spoon

A strainer

A large bowl

A paring knife

A cutting board

A grater

A fruit juicer

A food processor

A spoon

Veggie quinoa salad

Quick-cooking quinoa is a versatile whole grain that is packed with nutrients. You can use it in place of oatmeal for a warm breakfast, add it to something sweet for dessert, or make it savory like this Veggie Quinoa Salad. It is the only grain that is a complete protein, which means it's just as good for vegetarians as meat, chicken, and fish. It's also a very good source of magnesium, an important mineral for bone- and heart-health. An added bonus is that it is gluten-free.

Ingredients

¹⁄₃ cup chopped walnuts

1 tbsp olive oil

1 shallot

1 medium red bell pepper

1 small orange bell pepper

2 scallions

1 cup dry quinoa

2 cups low-sodium broth or water

¹⁄₂ cup golden raisins

3 tbsp lemon juice

Zest of 1 lemon

Salt and freshly ground black pepper

1. Place the sauté pan over medium–high heat and add the walnuts. Toast, letting your child shake the pan back and forth, for 3–5 minutes, until the nuts smell fragrant, but are not burning. Transfer to a small bowl and set aside.

2. Finely chop the onions and peppers. Add the oil to the pan and when hot, add the shallots. Sauté for about 2 minutes and then add the peppers. Sauté for another 5 minutes, stirring occasionally, until the peppers are soft but not mushy. Add the scallions to the pan and stir for a final minute. Turn off the heat and set the vegetables aside.

3 Let your child pour the dry quinoa into a medium pot and cover with water. Make sure he gives the quinoa a swirl in the water, and let it rest for about 5 minutes. Then he can pour it into a strainer and rinse off with cold water.

4 Transfer the quinoa back to the pot and cover with 2 cups of broth or water. Bring to a boil and then reduce to a simmer and cook for about 15 minutes, until the water is absorbed.

5 While the quinoa is cooking, have your child pour the raisins into a small bowl. Cover them with boiling water to plump them. Set aside for about 5–10 minutes and then drain the water.

6 Transfer the quinoa to a large mixing bowl. Help your child add the sautéed vegetables, walnuts, raisins, lemon juice, and lemon zest. Mix together to combine well, adding salt and pepper to taste, and serve.

Equipment

A medium sauté pan

2 small bowls

A paring knife

A cutting board

A spatula

A medium pot

A strainer

A large mixing bowl

Discovering different breads

Wherever you are in the world, chances are that bread, in one form or another, is a basic part of your diet, and these days our supermarket shelves are filled with all sorts of different types of bread. Children are often fixed on white bread, one of the least healthy varieties, but by creating a game with this simple tasting activity you can encourage them to try and eat different varieties.

Say to your child that you've bought some rolls and you need her help to find out which one makes the best sandwiches.

Cut a few slices off each one of the rolls or loaves and let her help you spread each one with her chosen topping. Place a slice of each type of bread on both plates, then place one plate in front of your child and the other in front of you.

Take turns trying bites of each of the types of bread. Ask her which one she prefers and why, and tell her which ones you prefer as well. Then help her put on the blindfold, and let her taste each of the breads again. See if she can guess which one she is eating, ask her which her favorite one is again, and see if it is the same type as before.

You will need

An assortment of at least 4 different types of soft rolls or small loaves, such as white, brown, whole-wheat, and seeded

Your child's favorite topping, such as soft cheese or jelly

A board

A butter knife for cutting and spreading

Two plates

A sleep mask or a scarf

Mac 'n' cheese

Macaroni and cheese is definitely a kid favorite! Boxed varieties may be quick to make, but it's not the same as the real deal, which can be made healthier. When it comes to grains, it's important to try to make half your choices whole grains. By substituting whole-wheat pasta for regular pasta in this recipe, you're getting a few servings of whole grains without taking away from the decadence of the dish. Plus, you'll get the added benefit of fiber, which will keep your children satisfied and prevent them from going back for seconds.

1 Preheat the oven to 350°F. Let your child spray the baking pan with cooking spray and set aside.

2 Bring a large pot of unsalted water to a boil, add the pasta, and cook, according to the package instructions, until it is just tender (al dente). Drain the pasta using a strainer (do not rinse it), and pour it back into the pot.

3 While the pasta is cooking, melt the butter in a large saucepan over a low heat. Mince the garlic and add to the saucepan, stir for 1–2 minutes.

4 Let your child add the cornstarch, mustard, salt, and chili pepper to the saucepan, and give him the whisk to stir the ingredients together until the mixture forms a thick paste.

Ingredients

Nonstick cooking spray

1 lb whole-wheat fusilli or penne

1 medium garlic clove

2 tbsp butter

1–2 tbsp cornstarch

1 ½ tbsp Dijon mustard

½ tsp salt

⅛ tsp chili powder

1 ½ cups skim milk

2 ½ cups shredded 2% reduced-fat cheddar cheese

½ cup grated Parmesan cheese

Equipment:

A 9 x 13-inch baking pan

A large pot

A strainer

A large saucepan

A wooden spoon

A whisk

5 Then he can slowly pour in the milk, while you show him how to stir vigorously to keep the sauce smooth. Continue cooking and stirring, for about 5 minutes until the sauce is smooth and thickened. Remove the pot from the heat.

6 Give your child the shredded cheddar cheese and half of the grated Parmesan cheese to add to the sauce, and have him stir until the cheese is melted and blended. Make sure there are no lumps.

7 Pour the cheese sauce over the pasta in the large pot and let him stir the pasta and cheese sauce until everything is coated.

8 Transfer the mixture to the prepared baking pan, and top with the rest of the Parmesan. Bake uncovered for about 20 minutes, until the edges are bubbly and the top is golden.

Helpful hint

If you prefer a cheesier version of mac 'n' cheese, you can just add more cheddar cheese to the sauce, in step 6.

Hummus and veggie pita

2 servings

Hummus is commonly used as a dip, but there's no reason you can't use it as a sandwich spread. Made from ground chickpeas, it's a good source of protein, magnesium (which is important for keeping muscles strong), and complex carbohydrates and folate, both of which help you maintain energy throughout the day.

1. If using a large pita, cut it in half widthways. If using two small pitas, cut each pita half way open.

2. Help your child spread a tablespoon of hummus on the inside of each pita.

3. Chop the vegetables—you should end up with 2 cups of chopped vegetables in total—and combine in one bowl.

4. Then let your child stuff each pita with half of the lettuce and a cup of vegetables of her liking. Top the vegetables with another tablespoon of hummus before serving.

Ingredients

1 large whole-wheat pita (6-inch diameter) or 2 small whole-wheat pitas (4-inch diameter)

1/4 cup hummus

1 medium carrot

1/2 bell pepper

1/2 cucumber

1/2 cup mushrooms

6 leaves of lettuce

Equipment

A bread knife

A plastic knife or spoon

Pouring and measuring

Cooking is a great way to introduce children to a series of practical hands-on skills. A pouring action, for example, is an easy uncomplicated movement for an adult but for a child, learning how to pour requires intense concentration and hand–eye coordination.

You will need

4 clear plastic pitchers

A tray

A package of dried beans or lentils

3 jars or jugs that are clear and of a similar size

A few drops of food coloring

Put the pitchers on the tray and fill one of them about a third full with beans or lentils. Then pick up that pitcher, supporting it with your other hand, and pour it into a second pitcher.

Ask your child to try the same motion. You may need to help her keep her hands steady the first couple of times. Once she has become confident pouring the beans, start to use finer substances, such as rice or sand, and then you can let her try with liquid.

At that point you can also start to introduce your child to terms of measurement. Fill one jug with water, and add some drops of food coloring, so that she can clearly see the levels, then pour the water into the other jugs, filling them to different levels, and ask her to find the jar that is full, the one that is empty and the one that is half full.

When she is familiar with these, let her practice pouring out these amounts, and when she has the hang of basic measurement terms, try introducing her to more precise measurements, such as one, half, and quarter cups.

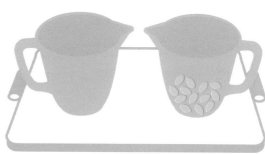

Veggie fried rice

8 servings

Just because fried rice has the word "fried" in it, doesn't mean it can't be healthy. This version of fried rice is made with healthy brown rice. Since it is not processed, brown rice is a rich source of fiber and other nutrients such as magnesium, zinc, and B vitamins.

1. Cook the rice in the pot according to package directions and let cool.

2. Chop the onion, broccoli, and mushrooms, and shred the carrot and cabbage with the help of your child. Then have him combine these in a large bowl, along with the edamame beans.

3. Heat a tablespoon of oil in the skillet or wok, over medium heat, then add the eggs, and scramble, allowing your child to help. Transfer the scrambled eggs to a plate and set aside until needed.

4. Add another tablespoon of oil to the skillet. When hot, add the cooked rice and stir to coat the grains. Continue stirring while your child adds the soy sauce and broth. Then add the rest of the oil and add the vegetables.

5. When the vegetables are cooked but still crunchy, add the eggs back to the skillet and stir until the eggs are hot and combined. Transfer to a plate and serve.

Ingredients

1 cup dry brown rice

1 medium onion

½ cup broccoli florets

4 mushrooms

6 oz of carrots

6 oz of purple cabbage

½ cup frozen edamame beans, shelled

3 tbsp canola or sesame oil

2 eggs

4 tbsp low-sodium soy sauce

4 tbsp low-sodium vegetable or chicken broth

Equipment

A pot

A paring knife

A cutting board

1 large bowl

1 large nonstick skillet or wok

1 large stirring spoon

A plate

5 Meat, chicken, fish, and tofu

Meat, poultry, and fish provide us with protein, iron, and zinc, while tofu is a great source of vegetarian protein and of iron and calcium. Use lean meat whenever possible, and trim off fat and skin. Baking or broiling are the healthiest cooking options for these foods—if you are frying the ingredients, do so lightly in just a little oil.

Turkey and cheese roll-ups

This recipe is so easy to make that your kids can do it all by themselves. Turkey breast is an excellent source of lean protein, but be careful what you purchase. Smoked turkey is full of added sodium, which can dehydrate children. The best thing to buy is fresh off-the-bone roasted turkey breast.

1. Have your child place one slice of turkey on a plate, and then top that with one slice of cheese.

2. Next, she can put one cucumber stick at one end of the cheese.

3. Starting from the end with the cucumber stick, show her how to roll up the turkey and cheese. (The cucumber should end up in the middle of the roll up.) If it doesn't stay rolled up, use a toothpick to secure.

4. Repeat steps 1 to 3 with the other slices, and then serve turkey roll-ups with mustard for dipping.

Ingredients

2 slices (about 2 oz) roasted turkey breast

2 slices (about 2 oz) reduced-fat Swiss or American cheese

2 cucumber sticks

2 teaspoons mustard

Equipment

A plate

A small dipping bowl

Helpful hint

This method can also be used to create roll-up sandwiches. Cut the crusts off a slice of bread and then layer the ingredients on top, and roll up as above.

Using your nose

Although we "taste" with our mouths, our tongues are limited to the five basic tastes—sweet, sour, salty, bitter, and umami. The more complex tastes come from our sense of smell, which is one of our strongest senses. This activity will show your child that her sense of smell plays a major part in the taste of food.

You will need

A selection of foods with strong and contrasting flavors

Ask your child how she thinks she tastes her food, and she will probably reply that it is by using her mouth (or tongue). Then you can tell her that you are going to do an experiment to see if that is true.

Lay out the different foods in front of your child, and ask her to choose one to eat and to describe the taste.

When she has finished, ask her to try another piece of the same food, but this time ask her to squeeze her nose as she eats it. See if she notices a difference in the taste. Try this with the other foods you have selected. You could use a blindfold as well as she tastes the food, as this often helps them to focus on the taste.

When she has tried all of the foods, ask her why she thinks the food tasted different with her nose blocked, when she wasn't able to use her sense of smell. Explain that when your nose is blocked and you can't use your sense of smell, your ability to taste is limited.

Steak fajitas

Bring a little Mexican flavor into your home with these quick and easy fajitas that will get the whole family involved! Lean steak is a great source of iron, an important nutrient for growing children, and the colorful veggies will ensure your kids get even more nutrients.

1. Mince the garlic, and help your child to juice the limes.

2. In a medium bowl, let him then combine the cinnamon, cumin, chilli powder, garlic, lime juice, and olive oil, and stir with a fork or whisk.

3. Cut the steak into 4 or 5 pieces. Add the steak to the bowl and help your child coat the pieces with the spice mixture. Set aside to marinate.

4. Next, slice the onion into half moons, and show him how to slice the peppers into strips using a plastic knife. In the meantime, cut the zucchini in half width-wise, and then slice it into strips lengthwise.

5. Spray a grill pan with cooking spray and place over medium–high heat. Add the steak and cook for 3–5 minutes per side until cooked as desired. Remove the steak to a carving board and leave to rest for about 5–10 minutes.

6. Coat a sauté pan with oil and place over medium-high heat. Add the vegetables and sauté until soft (about

Ingredients

2 garlic cloves

2 limes

$\frac{1}{4}$ tsp cinnamon

$\frac{1}{4}$ tsp cumin

2 tsp chili powder

2 tbsp olive oil

1 lb flank steak or top sirloin

1 medium onion

1 medium red pepper

1 medium yellow pepper

1 zucchini

Nonstick cooking spray

1 avocado

8 (6-inch) corn tortillas

2–3 plum tomatoes, diced

4 tbsp shredded Cheddar cheese (optional)

Cilantro, minced (optional)

5 minutes). Place the vegetables in a serving bowl and cover to keep them warm.

(7) Cut open the avocado, remove the pit, and show your child how to scoop out the avocado flesh into a medium bowl. Using a fork, let him mash the avocado until there are no big chunks left. Add 1 or 2 teaspoons of lime juice and let him continue stirring until well combined.

(8) Slice the steak thinly, and put on a serving plate.

(9) Warm the tortillas by putting them on the sauté pan for 30 seconds, turning once. Place on a serving dish in the center of the table.

(10) Dice the tomatoes, and then let your child place the tomatoes and cheese into small serving dishes.

(11) Show your child how to make his own fajitas by placing some mashed avocado on the tortilla, top with 2 or 3 slices of steak, and then layer with sautéed vegetables, tomato, cheese, and cilantro if desired. Fold over the sides and enjoy!

Equipment

Knife

A cutting board

A hand juicer

2 medium mixing bowls

Fork or whisk

Cutting board

A plastic knife

Grill pan

Tongs

Sauté pan

Serving bowls

Helpful hint

Some people think cilantro tastes like soap—there may be a genetic predisposition to disliking it. So keep in mind that it's a commonly disliked herb if your kids don't like it.

Salmon and vegetable kebabs

4
servings

Salmon is a heart-healthy fish that is good for skin, hair, and developing brains. It is an excellent source of omega-3 fatty acids, a very healthy type of unsaturated fat.

1. Cut the salmon fillet into cubes, about 2-inches big. Let your child season with salt and pepper.

2. Chop the pepper, onion, and zucchini into chunks, then mince the garlic and grate the ginger.

3. In a small bowl, let your child make the sauce by mixing together the maple syrup, soy sauce, cider vinegar, ginger, and garlic.

4. She can then place the salmon, vegetables, and pineapple in a medium bowl, and pour about three-quarters of the sauce over them. Cover the bowl with plastic wrap and refrigerate for 30 minutes. Meanwhile soak the wooden skewers in water for 30 minutes.

5. Then help her to thread alternating pieces of salmon and vegetables onto the skewers.

6. Spray the grill pan with cooking spray and heat over medium-high. When hot, place the skewers on the pan and grill for 10 to 15 minutes, rotating the skewers as they cook, until cooked as desired.

Ingredients

1 lb skinless salmon fillet

Salt and freshly ground black pepper

$^1/_3$ cup maple syrup

$^1/_3$ cup soy sauce

2 tbsp cider vinegar

$^1/_2$-inch piece of ginger

2 garlic cloves

1 large bell pepper

1 large onion

1 zucchini

1 cup fresh pineapple chunks

Nonstick cooking spray

Equipment

A cutting board

A chef's knife

A small bowl

A whisk or fork

A medium bowl

Plastic wrap

8–12 wooden skewers

Grill pan

Tongs

Baked chicken fingers

4 servings

Kids love chicken nuggets and crispy fingers, but they are not always the healthiest choice. These chicken fingers are made with 100 percent white chicken meat to keep it lean, and using whole-wheat panko bread crumbs adds fiber. Panko are Japanese bread crumbs and they have half the calories and one-tenth the sodium of traditional Italian bread crumbs. Plus, they are lighter and coarser than regular bread crumbs, which helps keep your "fried" food healthier because they don't absorb as much oil and fat, and they stay crisp after cooking.

1. Preheat the oven to 350°F. Let your child spray the baking sheet with cooking spray and set aside.

2. Mince the garlic and then have your child combine the panko, garlic, oregano, rosemary, salt, and pepper in one shallow bowl. Make sure the herbs are spread throughout the bread crumb mix.

3. Add the egg whites to a second shallow bowl, and let your child whisk the eggs (either with a whisk or fork).

4. Slice the chicken breasts into even strips (you should have about 16 strips in total).

Ingredients

Nonstick cooking spray

1 ½ cups whole-wheat panko bread crumbs

1 medium-sized garlic clove

1 ½ tsp fresh oregano or ½ tsp dried

1 ½ tsp fresh rosemary or ½ tsp dried

¼ tsp salt

¼ tsp freshly ground black pepper

2 egg whites

1 lb boneless chicken breast

¼ cup Dijon mustard

¼ cup honey

Splash of orange juice

5. Show your child how to dip a strip of chicken into the egg whites to coat all sides, and then to transfer the strip to the panko-herb mixture and coat it well. Remove the chicken from the bread crumbs, shaking off any excess coating.

6. Place the chicken strip on the baking sheet, then help him continue to coat the rest of the chicken strips.

7. Once all the strips have been coated and placed on the baking sheet, place the baking sheet in the oven and cook for 15–20 minutes (depending on the thickness of the chicken). Flip the chicken strips halfway through the cooking time.

8. While the chicken strips are baking, prepare the dipping sauce. Let your child add the mustard, honey, and orange juice to a mixing bowl, and then whisk together until all ingredients are combined and the sauce is the consistency of syrup. Set aside in a small bowl.

9. Serve the chicken fingers hot from the oven with the dipping sauce.

Equipment

A baking sheet

2 shallow bowls

A cutting board

A chef's knife

Measuring cups

Measuring spoons

A medium-sized mixing bowl

A whisk or fork

Making table settings

Today's busy lifestyle means that there's not always time for a family dinner around the table, but it's a great way to spend time together. This activity encourages children to help prepare for meal times, and get familiar with basic table settings and manners.

Center the plate in the middle of one piece of card, rim side down. Holding the plate steady, ask your child to draw carefully around the plate with the pencil.

Then place the cutlery around the plate tracing in the usual place setting: the knife on the right, fork on the left, and the spoon above. Let her draw around these as well.

Show her that you've made a table setting guide, so that she can help you to set the table for dinner. Ask her to set an actual place setting using the drawing as a guide.

As she becomes more confident, let her try without using the guide, and start to introduce more tableware items, one or two at a time, such as napkins, cups, and soup spoons.

As an added bit of fun, you can also help her to make up a menu for the evening. Fold the other sheet of card widthways, so that the card can stand up. Let her choose a name for her "restaurant," then help her to write the name on the front of the card, and list what you're having for dinner on the inside. Let her decorate it with drawings and pictures and place it on the table, ready for dinner.

You will need

1 dinner plate

2 sheets of light colored card, A4 size or bigger

A set of cutlery including a knife, fork, and dessert spoon

1 pencil

1 black felt-tipped pen

Coloring pencils

Chicken Negimaki

4 servings

Negimaki is a traditional Japanese dish made of thin strips of beef marinated in teriyaki sauce wrapped around scallions and broiled. This version is made using thinly pounded chicken breast to keep it leaner and lighter for your family. You can make the marinade as in the recipe or use bottled teriyaki sauce to save time. Either way this dish will be delicious!

1. In a mixing bowl, have your child mix together the soy sauce, rice vinegar, sesame oil, garlic, and ginger.

2. Show him how to pound the chicken breasts to ¼-inch thickness using a smooth meat mallet or a rolling pin. Then cut each breast widthwise into 3 pieces, and cut the scallions into pieces about 3 inches long.

3. Place 1 or 2 chunks of scallions on the narrow end of a chicken piece, roll the chicken up, and use a toothpick to secure. Let your child repeat with the remaining chicken and scallion pieces.

4. Place the roll ups in the marinade, cover with plastic wrap and refrigerate for 30 minutes.

5. Preheat the oven to 350°F. Line a baking sheet with aluminum foil and set aside.

Ingredients

For the Chicken

¼ cup low sodium soy sauce

2 tbsp rice vinegar

2 tsp sesame oil

1 tbsp minced garlic

1 tbsp freshly grated ginger

1 ½ lbs of boneless, skinless chicken breast

1 bunch scallions, trimmed

1 tbsp canola oil

For the Dipping Sauce

¼ cup low sodium soy sauce

¼ cup honey

½ cup rice vinegar

2 tsp cornstarch dissolved in 2 tbsp water

6 Heat 1 tablespoon of oil in a skillet over a medium-high heat and then cook the chicken pieces in batches for 5–6 minutes, turning once, until they are all well-browned.

7 Transfer the cooked chicken pieces to the baking sheet and cook in the oven until they are cooked through, about 10 minutes.

8 To make the dipping sauce, in a small saucepan, have your child combine the soy sauce, honey, vinegar, and the dissolved cornstarch.

9 Bring to a boil and stir constantly until it reaches a syrup consistency. Place in a bowl and serve with the chicken.

Equipment

A large mixing bowl

A meat mallet or rolling pin

A whisk or fork

A knife

A cutting board

Toothpicks

Plastic wrap

A baking sheet

Aluminum foil

A large skillet

A small saucepan

A stirring spoon

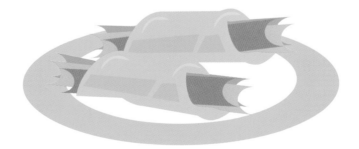

Fish sticks

Most store-bought fish sticks are tasty, but full of fat and additives. This healthy homemade version is almost as easy to make as frozen ones, and you'll feel even better about serving them.

1. In a shallow bowl, have your child mix together the bread crumbs and Parmesan cheese. Add Old bay or Cajun seasoning for more flavor if desired.

2. In another shallow bowl, let her crack the egg and beat it with a fork or whisk.

3. Slice the fish into wide strips, about 1½-ounces each. Then, show your child how to dip a strip in the egg, let the excess drip off, then roll it in the bread crumbs. Set it aside on a plate and let her continue coating the rest.

4. Cut the lemon in half and show her how to squeeze the juice into a small bowl. Set aside.

5. In the skillet, melt 1 tablespoon of the butter over a medium heat. When hot, place the fish strips in the pan and cook on one side until they are brown, about 2–3 minutes. Pour 1 tablespoon of the lemon juice over the fish and then cook it for another minute.

6. Carefully flip the fish strips. Add the rest of the butter if needed, and repeat step 5.

7. Place on a plate and serve with either tartar sauce or cocktail sauce.

Ingredients

1 cup Italian-style bread crumbs

¼ cup grated Parmesan cheese

1 tsp Old bay or Cajun seasoning (optional)

1 egg

1½ lbs sole or other white fish fillets

1 lemon

1–2 tbsp butter or trans-fat free margarine

½ cup tartar sauce or cocktail sauce, to serve

Equipment

2 shallow bowls

A whisk or fork

A knife

A cutting board

A plate

A small bowl

A large nonstick skillet

A spatula

Where do we keep that?

Young children don't yet know that certain food needs to be kept in the fridge, while others can stay in the cupboard, or that some need to be kept in airtight containers, while others can be kept loose. This activity will show them that, and introduce them to the fact that food goes bad, so it needs to be stored correctly.

You will need

A variety of foods from your weekly household shopping (loose fruit or veg, milk, glass jars, cans, etc.)

With the different foods and packaging laid out in front of you both, explain to your child that he is going to help you sort out the weekly shopping into groups, by their different food packaging.

Ask him to put all the canned goods together, then the packets, the glass jars, loose bagged vegetables, and so on, until all of the items have been sorted into a group.

Go through each group in turn, asking him to tell you what each container has in it. Ask him where he thinks each item should be stored—the fridge, freezer, or store cupboard. Point out any clues that appear on the packaging to help him if he needs it.

Then ask him questions to show him the link between the packaging and the type of food, such as, "Why do we put tomatoes in the fridge but not a can of beans?" What does he think will happen if the milk isn't kept in the fridge?

Meat, chicken, fish, and tofu 101

Spaghetti bolognese

Spaghetti bolognese is a firm kid's favorite. There's plenty of flavor and nutrients from the the tomatoes, mushrooms, onions, and herbs. For an even healthier option, you could use lean, ground turkey to reduce the saturated fat.

1. Chop the onions and mushrooms, and mince the garlic. Heat 1 tablespoon of oil in the pot over medium-high heat. Add the beef and cook, stirring occasionally and breaking it up into small pieces, for about 5 to 7 minutes, until the meat is no longer pink.

2. Using a slotted spoon, let your child transfer the meat to a bowl and set aside. Use a paper towel to wipe out any fat left in the pot.

3. Heat the rest of the oil in the pot over a medium-high heat. Add the onions and mushrooms and cook, stirring occasionally, for about 5–7 minutes. Then add the garlic and herbs and cook for another 5 minutes.

4. Help your child open the can of tomatoes and pour the contents into the pot. Then help her add the cooked beef, water, and tomato paste.

5. Bring the sauce to a boil, then simmer, covered on a medium-low heat, stirring occasionally, for 30 minutes. Season with salt and pepper, serve with spaghetti.

Ingredients

1 medium onion

$\frac{1}{2}$ lb white mushrooms

3 garlic cloves

2 tbsp olive oil

1–1$\frac{1}{4}$ lb lean ground beef

2 tsp dried basil

1 tsp dried oregano

$\frac{1}{2}$ tsp dried thyme

1 (28-oz) can tomatoes

$\frac{1}{2}$ cup water

3 tbsp tomato paste

Salt and freshly ground black pepper

Whole-wheat spaghetti, cooked according to packet

Equipment

A knife

A cutting board

A large pot

A spatula

A slotted spoon

A bowl

Paper towels

Measuring spoons

Apple-cranberry tuna salad

4 servings

Get some extra fruit into your children's diet, by adding crunchy apples and dried cranberries to a tradiditonal tuna salad. Tuna is an excellent source of lean protein and heart-healthy omega-3 fatty acids, but it is also high in mercury. Canned chunk light tuna is lower in mercury, and therefore a better choice.

1. If your child is able, let him open the cans of tuna, using a can opener.

2. Help him drain the tuna and add it to a small mixing bowl. He can then mash the tuna using a fork.

3. Chop the shallot and let your child add it and the mayonnaise to the tuna, and continue to mash to combine the ingredients.

4. Next, chop the apple into small pieces. Cut the lemon in half, and show your child how to juice it.

5. Let him add the apples and cranberries and toss to combine into the tuna, and then add about 2½ tablespoons of lemon juice into the tuna salad, add a few turns of pepper, and again toss to combine.

6. Serve either on bread as a sandwich, on top of salad, or just by itself.

Ingredients

2 (5-oz) cans of chunk light tuna fish, canned in water

1 shallot

2 tbsp light mayonnaise

¼ apple (preferably crunchy)

1 lemon

¼ cup dried cranberries

Freshly ground black pepper

Equipment

A can opener

A small mixing bowl

A fork

A knife

A cutting board

A lemon squeezer

Measuring spoons

My own cookbook

Here's a chance for your child to create his very own cookbook, and fill it with all the first recipes that he makes, as well as ones collected from friends, family, magazines, and the Internet.

Ask your child to think of a name that he would like for his cookbook and, if he is able, let him write it on the cover (or you write it). Let him select some food pictures that he likes, cut them out, and arrange them on the cover. Once he is happy with the arrangement he can glue the pictures down.

When the cover is finished, help him to cut the sticky plastic out to the size of the book, and then wrap it around the cover to seal it.

Together you can decide the order of the recipes—by food group, alphabetically, or by course— and then divide the book equally with a heading for each section.

Help him to collect, cut out or write and stick in recipes gathered from all available sources that you can try out together, and he can keep it forever as a treasured memory of his first attempts at cooking.

You will need

An empty lined notebook, preferably A4

Old magazines with pictures of food

A pair of scissors

A glue stick

Sticky plastic for covering

A pencil

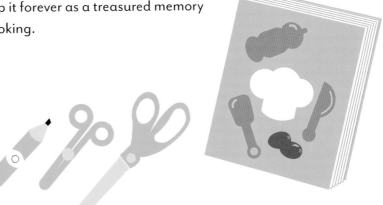

Tofu stir-fry

Tofu is made from the curds of soybean milk and is a great source of vegetarian protein, and of iron and calcium, two minerals that are very important for growing kids.

1. Cut open the tofu package and help your child drain it.

2. Using a plastic knife, help your child cut the tofu into 10–12 portions, and then place them between a few layers of paper towels to soak up the moisture. Set aside for 15 minutes to an hour.

3. Slice the onion into half moons, the pepper into strips, and chop the broccoli. Let your child rinse off the string beans and snap off the ends. Peel the carrot and then slice thinly.

4. Heat the oil in the wok over a high heat. Add the tofu and cook until it is golden brown, about 1–2 minutes per side. Remove from the pan and set aside.

5. Spray the pan with cooking spray, add the onions. Cook for about 5 minutes, stirring continuously. Then add the broccoli, pepper, and carrot and cook for another 3–5 minutes. Add the green beans or snow peas and cook for another minute, still stirring continuously.

6. Finally, add the tofu and the stir-fry sauce and stir to coat everything. Serve hot over rice.

Ingredients

1 (16-oz) package firm or extra-firm tofu

1 medium onion

1 large yellow pepper

1 head of broccoli

½ lb string beans (or snow peas)

1 carrot

1 tbsp canola oil

Nonstick cooking spray

1 cup stir-fry sauce

Equipment

Scissors or a knife

A plastic knife

Paper towels

A cutting board

A peeler

A wok or large sauté pan

A spatula

6 Healthy treats

Children always seem to be drawn to the foods that are the least healthy for them, so trying to limit their intake of sweets and chocolate can be tricky. In moderation, the occasional sweet treat is fine, but there are also plenty of delicious recipes you can make that are healthier than traditional calorie-laden desserts, and sometimes just swapping out an ingredient in the recipe, like butter, can make a treat that little bit healthier.

Oatmeal cranberry raisin cookies

24 cookies

Not many cookies can boast health benefits, but these can. Oats and whole wheat flour are full of fiber, and the dried fruit gives them a naturally sweet flavor and an antioxidant boost.

1. Preheat the oven to 375°F. Line 2 baking sheets with silicone mats (or baking paper covered with oil spray).

2. Help your child to measure out the flours, baking powder, baking soda, cinnamon, and salt, and then whisk them together in a small bowl.

3. In a large bowl, beat the butter spread and sugar until smooth, and then let your child mix in the brown sugar, egg, applesauce, and vanilla.

4. She can then add the dry ingredients to the large bowl. Mix together until there are no streaks of flour remaining, and then let her add the oats, raisins, and dried cranberries, and stir until everything is combined.

5. Show her how to drop teaspoons of batter 2 inches apart onto the baking sheets. Bake for 10–12 minutes or until golden brown but still soft in the center.

6. Remove from the oven and allow to cool for 5–10 minutes. Then transfer to a wire rack to cool.

Ingredients

$\frac{1}{2}$ cup all-purpose flour

$\frac{1}{2}$ cup whole-wheat flour

1 tsp baking powder

$\frac{1}{2}$ tsp baking soda

$\frac{1}{2}$ tsp ground cinnamon

$\frac{1}{4}$ teaspoon salt

2 tbsp light butter spread or trans-fat free margarine

$\frac{1}{2}$ cup granulated sugar

$\frac{1}{2}$ cup packed brown sugar

1 large egg

$\frac{1}{4}$ cup unsweetened applesauce

1 tsp vanilla extract

1$\frac{1}{3}$ cup rolled oats

$\frac{1}{3}$ cup raisins

$\frac{1}{3}$ cup dried cranberries

Equipment

2 large baking sheets

Silicone mats

A wooden spoon

A small bowl

A whisk or fork

A large bowl

Carrot muffins

12 muffins

Carrot muffins are an excellent source of vitamin A, which helps keep your eyes healthy and the fiber in whole-wheat flour also keeps your digestive tract working properly.

1. Preheat the oven to 350°F. Let your child place the muffin liners in the muffin tin and spray well with cooking spray. Set aside.

2. In a large bowl, help your child mix together the flours, sugar, baking powder, baking soda, salt, cinnamon, nutmeg, and ginger.

3. In a medium bowl, let him whisk together the eggs, oil, applesauce, and vanilla, and then fold the wet mixture into the large bowl, stirring well to combine.

4. Show him how to grate the carrots (you should end up with 2 cups of grated carrot). Fold into the mixture.

5. With your child's help, spoon the batter into the muffin cups (about two-thirds full). Bake for 25–30 minutes, until a toothpick inserted in the center comes out clean. Remove from oven and let cool for 5 minutes, then remove from the tin and cool on a wire rack.

Ingredients

Nonstick cooking spray

3/4 cup whole-wheat flour

3/4 cup all purpose flour

2/3 cup brown sugar, packed

1 tsp baking powder

1/2 tsp baking soda

1/4 tsp salt

1 1/2 tsp ground cinnamon

1/4 tsp nutmeg

1/4 tsp ginger

2 large eggs

1/4 cup vegetable oil

1/2 cup unsweetened applesauce

1 tsp vanilla extract

4 medium carrots

Equipment

12-cup muffin tin and liners

A large mixing bowl

A medium mixing bowl

A fork or whisk

A grater

A spatula

A spoon

A sugar experiment

This is a fun but simple experiment that kids will love to try, but hopefully it will also make them more aware of why too much sugar in our diets is bad for us, especially for our teeth, and should only be a small part of our diet.

Show your child the marble chips, and explain that the chips represent your teeth (if your child has lost a tooth recently, you could use that as well). Ask him what he thinks will happen to them if they are left in each of the different liquids that you have, and then tell him you're going to do an experiment to find out.

Fill each jar with a small amount of one of the liquids, enough to submerge the marble chip, and then place a chip in each one. The liquids should be kept in airtight jars to stop mold from forming, but be careful when opening the jar containing the fizzy drink as gas pressure may build up.

Over the course of the next 4 to 5 days, ask your child to check daily to look at the size of the marble pieces, and see what happens. He can record the results in a log. The one in the fizzy drink should disappear completely.

Ask your child what they think may have happened, and explain that food and sugar form into an acid that eats into your tooth and gums, and that's why it's important not to eat too much of it. And why he should always brush his teeth!

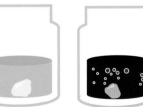

Mango lassi ice pops

4 pops

Mango lassi is a popular Indian drink. In this recipe, the typical mango lassi has been made into ice pops. It is a healthy variation to the regular ice pops you'll find at the grocery store. Mango is an excellent source of vitamins A and C, and the probiotics in plain yogurt can help keep the immune system strong (look for the label that says "live with active cultures"), and of course, calcium found in yogurt and milk is essential for bone health.

Ingredients

1 ripe mango

½ cup fat-free plain yogurt

2 tbsp skim milk

1 tbsp honey

Equipment

A plastic or dull knife

A cutting board

A food processor or blender

4 ice pop molds

1. Peel the mango and remove the seed, then help your child dice the flesh using a plastic or dull knife, until you have 1 cup of mango pieces.

2. Let her put the diced mango into the food processor or blender, and then add the yogurt, milk, and honey.

3. Blend all ingredients until well combined and then help your child to pour the mixture into molds. Freeze until firm and ready to eat.

4. To remove the ice pops from the mold, show your child how to run warm water over the molds until you are able to detach the ice pop from the container.

Chocolate pudding cups

Chocolate pudding is a decadent treat all kids seem to love. But why buy the packaged varieties when you can easily make it yourself at home? Kids will be amazed how the pudding thickens from start to finish, and parents will be thrilled that one pudding cup counts as one serving of bone-building calcium! Unsweetened cocoa powder and 60–70 percent cacao chocolate chunks make this pudding very rich, but it also provides you with a good dose of antioxidants called flavonols.

1. Let your child measure out the sugar, cornstarch, cocoa, and salt, and add them to a medium saucepan (off the heat). Then let him stir the ingredients together with a whisk.

2. Help him to gradually add the evaporated milk to the dry ingredients, stirring with a whisk to combine.

3. Once all of the evaporated milk is added and the mixture is liquid, he can also add the low-fat milk and stir with a whisk.

4. Place the saucepan over medium–high heat and stir constantly with a whisk—your child can help if she is able—until it comes to a boil (about 5–7 minutes).

5. Reduce the heat, and simmer for about 1–2 minutes, continuing to stir, until thick.

Ingredients

⅓ cup granulated sugar

3 tbsp cornstarch

2 tbsp unsweetened cocoa

⅛ tsp salt

1 (12-oz) can evaporated fat-free milk

1 cup nonfat or 1% low-fat milk

2 oz semisweet chocolate chunks (60 to 70% cacao)

1 tsp vanilla extract

Whipped cream to serve (optional)

Equipment

A medium saucepan

A whisk

A ladle

4 (6-oz) ramekins

Plastic wrap or wax paper

6. Turn off the heat and have your child add the chocolate chunks, stirring until they are melted and the mixture is smooth. Then he can add the vanilla and stir to combine.

7. Using a ladle, pour about ½ cup of the pudding into each ramekin. Cover the surface of each pudding cup with plastic wrap, being sure to press the plastic wrap or wax paper against the chocolate to prevent a skin from forming. Refrigerate for at least 30 minutes.

8. Remove from the fridge and serve. For an extra treat you can add a dollop of whip cream.

What do I use that for?

Having the right tool for the job when cooking can make all the difference. When children first start to cook, the utensils and tools will be new to them, and it won't always be obvious which one does what. Making a simple pairing game out of it will help children to remember each tool.

Gather together a range of different vessels and utensils, and set them out in two separate groups (for younger children, start with only three matching items and introduce more gradually). See if your child can tell you the name of each one, and tell him any that he doesn't know.

Now you're going to get your child to be a cooking detective and try to match up the utensils to the right equipment. Let him choose one item, for example a saucepan. Then ask him a question to prompt him to pick out a matching utensil, such as, "If I was cooking potatoes in the pan and I wanted to mash them, what utensil do you think I would need?"

Hopefully he would then select the masher but if he is having difficulty give him a few clues like, "It has a long handle with a flat oval base with holes in it." Once he has matched the items correctly, continue with the rest of the equipment, until all of the items have been paired up.

Once he starts to get the hang of it, you can make the activity more challenging, and introduce terms such as heat resistant or nonstick, and discuss why each utensil is best for each of the jobs.

You will need

A selection of cooking vessels including pots, skillet, mixing bowls, jug

A selection of utensils to go with them like a fish slice, wooden spoon, balloon whisk, a metal spoon a potato masher, a sieve

Trail mix

Trail mix is a healthy, easy-to-make snack that you can pack in lunch boxes, or throw in a bag when on the go or traveling. What's great about this recipe is that you and your children can get creative and experiment with any combination of cereal, nuts, and dried fruit you have in your pantry. This trail mix will keep your children satisfied for hours because of the filling combo of carbohydrates, healthy fat, protein, and fiber. Plus, the chocolate chips are a great way to satisfy a sweet tooth!

1 Let your child measure out all of the ingredients, helping her if she needs it, and then place them all in a large bowl.

2 Give her the large spoon to mix all of the ingredients together well.

3 Separate a quarter of a cup of trail mix into each resealable bag. Store for an easy grab-and-go snack!

Ingredients

½ cup corn chex or rice chex (or similar cereal)

½ cup raw walnut halves

½ cup roasted, unsalted almonds

½ cup dried apples

2 tbsp raisins

2 tbsp dried cranberries

2 tbsp mini semisweet chocolate chips

Equipment

Measuring cups

Measuring spoons

1 large bowl

1 large spoon

8 resealable bags

Peanut butter blondies

12
blondies

Brownies and blondies are often filled with saturated fat. To reduce that, these blondies contain egg whites instead of whole eggs and most of the butter is replaced with applesauce. There is also a boost of whole grains and fiber from the whole-wheat flour.

1. Preheat the oven to 350°F. Coat an 8 x 8-inch square baking pan with nonstick cooking spray and set aside.

2. In a large mixing bowl, cream the peanut butter and butter together using an electric hand mixer. Help your child add the sugar, vanilla, egg whites, and applesauce while you continue beating the mixture until it becomes fluffy.

3. Using a wire whisk, your child can mix the whole-wheat flour, baking powder, cocoa powder, and salt in a medium mixing bowl. Then, he can slowly add the dry ingredients to the peanut butter mixture and mix until well blended.

4. Help your child spread the batter evenly into the prepared baking pan. Bake for 30 minutes. Then remove from the oven to cool. Once cooled, cut into 12 even squares (about 2 x 2 inches) and serve!

Ingredients

Nonstick cooking spray

$\frac{1}{2}$ cup all natural crunchy peanut butter

3 tbsp unsalted butter, softened

1 cup brown sugar, packed

1 tsp vanilla extract

$\frac{3}{4}$ cup egg whites (about 8 large egg whites)

2 tbsp unsweetened applesauce

$\frac{2}{3}$ cups whole-wheat or whole-wheat white flour

1 tsp baking powder

1 tsp unsweetened cocoa powder

$\frac{1}{4}$ tsp salt

Equipment

An 8 x 8-inch baking pan

A large mixing bowl

An electric hand mixer

A wire whisk

A medium mixing bowl

Baked apples

4 servings

Apple pie, apple crisp, apple tart—all these desserts are delicious, but they are definitely special occasion treats. Not so with baked apples, which still have the same warm, delicious flavors, and are a great way to fit a fruit serving into your child's daily intake.

1. Preheat the oven to 350°F.

2. Peel the top of the apples, and show your child how to core them using an apple corer (or use a paring knife to remove the stem area and use a spoon to remove the rest of the core). Make sure to leave the bottom intact.

3. Have your child rub the lemon on the tops of the apples where they were peeled. She can also squeeze some juice in the core area that is now empty.

4. In a small bowl, she can then combine the brown sugar and cinnamon, and spoon equal amounts of the mixture into each of the apples.

5. Pour water into the baking pan and place the apples in the pan. Let your child drizzle the syrup over all of the apples. Cover with foil and bake for about 50 minutes.

6. Remove from the oven. Serve with vanilla ice cream for an extra treat.

Ingredients

4 cooking apples

½ lemon

2 tbsp brown sugar

½ tsp cinnamon

½ cup water

1 tbsp maple syrup

Vanilla ice cream, to serve (optional)

Equipment

A peeler

An apple corer

A small bowl

A spoon

An 8 x 8-inch baking pan

Aluminum foil

Chocolate covered pretzels

32 pretzels

These chocolate covered pretzels are a fun treat that parents and kids can easily make together. Dark chocolate adds great flavor and healthy antioxidants, but this recipe can also be made with semisweet milk chocolate or white chocolate chips. You can also experiment with different toppings: have fun with rolling your pretzels in different healthy toppings of their choice.

1. Place a sheet of wax paper on a large baking sheet and set aside.

2. If you are using toppings, have your child measure out ¼ cup of each topping and place on large plate.

3. Place 2 inches of water in the pot and heat until the water simmers. Then, put the chocolate in the bowl and place the bowl on top of the pot (don't let it touch the water). The steam will melt the chocolate.

4. Help your child carefully submerge pretzel twists in the melted chocolate, making sure they are coated on both sides. Then, fish out the pretzels with a fork.

5. Have your child roll the pretzels in toppings if desired. Then place on the wax paper and refrigerate for 15– 20 minutes, until the chocolate has hardened.

Ingredients

1 cup 65% bittersweet dark chocolate or semisweet chocolate chips

2 oz mini whole-wheat pretzel twists

Selection of optional toppings: chopped peanuts, coconut flakes, or dried cranberries

Equipment

Wax paper

A large baking sheet

A large plate for toppings (optional)

A pot

A glass bowl, larger than the pot

A stirring spoon

A fork

Picnic time

A picnic is an exciting event for a child, especially if you can pack up food that you have cooked or prepared together, such as Fruit Kebabs (see page 22), Turkey and Cheese Roll-ups (see page 88), or Oatmeal Cranberry Raisin Cookies (see page 110).

Preparing the picnic is as much fun as having it, so let your child help you select and prepare the foods you want to take with you. Make sure to include food that is practical to eat outside—finger foods are often best.

Pack up the food and drink into sealed containers, making sure nothing will leak, and then into one container or basket, with anything else you want to take with you, such as a blanket or sunshade.

Find a place outside that is quiet and safe for your picnic. It doesn't have to be adventurous—if you don't have a suitable park nearby, the backyard is fine. Spread out your blanket in your chosen spot and make sure you and your child are well protected from the sun.

Lay out all the food, and let your child try a little of each. Try to include something from each of the food groups, to encourage him to eat a well-balanced meal.

You will need

Picnic food and drink of your choice

Food containers

Cutlery and plates, preferably plastic, to take outdoors

A large basket or container

A blanket

A sunshade

Cute cupcakes

18 cupcakes

Cupcakes are a wonderful treat to have on any occasion. They're an ideal starting point for all budding bakers, offering your child the perfect opportunity to learn how to mix just the right amount of ingredients to create a delicious delight.

1. Preheat the oven to 350°F.

2. Put the butter and sugar into the large bowl. Show your child how to cream them with the wooden spoon until really soft. This will take about 5 minutes.

3. Show your child how to crack an egg by tapping it on the side of the bowl and pushing your thumbs into the egg shell to ease it open. Add the egg to the butter and sugar and let her stir it in with the wooden spoon. Then let her try to crack the next two eggs herself, adding them to the mixture one at a time.

4. Tip the flour into the bowl and pour in the milk. Gently stir everything together until the mixture is smooth.

5. Put 18 paper liners into the muffin tins and ask your child to put a big spoonful of the mixture into each one.

6. Bake the cupcakes in the oven for 15 minutes, until they are risen and golden brown.

Ingredients

²⁄₃ cup butter, at room temperature

³⁄₄ cup golden caster (superfine) sugar

3 eggs

1 cup self-rising flour

2 tbsp milk

1 cup raspberries

1 tbsp apple juice

2¹⁄₃ cups powdered sugar

Equipment

A large bowl

A wooden spoon

18 paper muffin liners

2 muffin tins

A tablespoon

A cup

A medium bowl

A fork

A sieve

A teaspoon

7. To make the topping, get your child to put the raspberries into a medium bowl and squish them together with a fork. Add the apple juice and mix.

8. Then show her how to sift the icing sugar into a bowl using a sieve. Add the crushed raspberries and apple juice and mix everything together.

9. Spoon and spread the icing on top of the cooled cupcakes.

Helpful hint

Using this recipe as your basis, finish with a flourish with these great topping ideas:

- Cut a cherry in half and place on top.
- Cover the icing with a layer of sprinkles.
- Add a dash of shredded coconut for a more exotic flavor.

Index